W9-BLZ-454

Neighborhood Planning

*A Guide
for
Citizens
and
Planners*

Neighborhood Planning

A Guide for Citizens and Planners

By
Bernie Jones

PLANNERS PRESS
AMERICAN PLANNING ASSOCIATION
Chicago, Illinois
Washington, D.C.

Excerpt from *Dateline America* by Charles Kuralt, copyright © 1979 by CBS, reprinted by permission of Harcourt Brace Jovanovich, Inc.

Copyright 1990 by the American Planning Association
122 S. Michigan Ave., Ste. 1600
Chicago, IL 60603
Paperback edition ISBN 0–918286–67–0
Hardbound edition ISBN 0–198286–68–9
Library of Congress Catalog Card Number 90–80549

Printed in the United States of America
All rights reserved

HALF PRICE BOOKS ®

Half Price Books
1835 Forms Drive
Carrollton, TX 75006
OFS OrderID 18906033

‖‖‖‖‖‖‖‖‖‖‖

Thank you for your order, Halo Books
WST_AG129196-68POWST_AG129196-68-1!

Thank you for shopping with Half Price Books! Please contact service19@hpb.com. if you have
any questions, comments or concerns about your order (113-7713195-0773868)

SKU	ISBN/UPC	Title & Author/Artist	Shelf ID	Qty	OrderSKU
S318712969	9780918286673	Neighborhood Planning: A Guide for Citizen... Jones, Bernie	A HIST 1.1	1	

ORDER# 113-7713195-0773868
AmazonMarketplaceUS

SHIPPED STANDARD TO:
Halo   Books
WST_AG129196-68POWST_AG129196-68-1
2711 West Ash Street
Columbia MO 65203
dwk8ykfgfbdllg5@marketplace.amazon.com

Acknowledgments

The author wishes to acknowledge the Center for Community Development and Design of the University of Colorado at Colorado Springs and its director, Bill Leon, for originally engaging me to prepare an earlier version of this guide.

Contents

Illustrations

A Word of Inspiration

Boston. During the Revolution, people in Boston used to say Sam Adams did the writing and John Hancock paid the postage. Brilliant Sam Adams and his wealthy friend Hancock were among the targets of the march of the Redcoats to Lexington and Concord. They were to be captured and tried for treason, of which they were unmistakably guilty. But they escaped and lived to see their country free. They are buried not far from each other in the same cemetery, a few steps from Boston Common. Robert Treat Paine, who also signed the Declaration of Independence, and James Otis, the fiery patriot who survived the Revolution only to be killed by lightning, lie in this same, small, tree-shaded place, the Old Granary Burying Ground. So does the black man Crispus Attucks and the others who were shot down by British soldiers in the Boston Massacre.

There are some patriots buried here of whom you may not have heard. One gravestone says, "Elisha Brown. He bravely and successfully opposed a whole British regiment in their violent attempts to force him from his legal habitation."

He *did*? Why, this Elisha Brown must have been quite a man! It turns out Elisha did it by buying a lot of groceries. When the British occupied Boston in 1769 and forced every householder to provide food and shelter to the British troops, Elisha Brown decided he wouldn't. He put in enough food for a year, barred his doors, locked his windows, and settled down for a long stay. His food held out longer than British patience. After a few weeks, they marked him down as a stubborn old fool and went away and left him alone.

This old graveyard is full of stubborn men. This one, a stone says, "was wounded by the enemy and died painfully of his wounds." This one died "opposing the British." It doesn't say how this man died, but we remember his name, and how stubborn Paul Revere was.

If you come to Boston, leave the busy street for a few minutes and walk into this quiet place. It's a good place to think.

The thought that crossed my mind was that all these men were neighbors. What a neighborhood!

Charles Kuralt
Dateline America
1979

How to Use This Guide

Two categories of users of this guide are contemplated: professional planners, most likely employed in city planning offices and citizen planners, that is, laypeople, without a planning background, who become involved in neighborhood planning. In the best of all possible worlds, both the professional and citizen planner would be using the guide together, as they jointly set about drafting a neighborhood plan.

While having that team approach in mind in preparing this guide, I have nevertheless tried to create a document that would be useful to both that team and to citizen planners working on their own. It is quite easy to imagine neighborhood residents doing a neighborhood plan on their own: it happens with increasing frequency these days. It is more difficult to imagine a neighborhood planner preparing a neighborhood plan without the residents being involved with the process. This book uses a democratic, participatory planning approach, and the planner working without the people has perhaps picked up the wrong book! It is this author's belief that laypeople, with determination and reasonable intelligence, can indeed produce a neighborhood plan. It is also my contention that neighborhood planning should be at the heart of what city planning offices do. The intent of this guide is to take some of the mystery out of that task for citizen and professional planner alike. Incidentally, the term *planning group* or planning team is used throughout the book to refer to residents working on their own or to residents and professionals working together.

Assuming it is a joint undertaking of professional and citizen planner, an integral part of the undertaking will be, or should be, the carving out of the relationship among themselves. What is most crucial here is being open and conscious of the roles and relationships. Who will be doing what should be spelled out at the start, but not etched in stone. Periodically, events may transpire that lead to reconsideration of the roles and relationships. This is increasingly important today as some planning offices are redefining the role of their neighborhood planners in the direction of more complexity. While in the past, neighborhood planners prepared plans, period, today they are as likely to be a conduit of information and a liaison with city agencies as well. Maintaining regular contact becomes even more important under these circumstances. Maintaining regular contact will not guarantee that things will not go wrong, but failing to maintain regular contact will almost certainly guarantee that many things will go wrong!

Neighborhood planners working with residents need to understand the enormous potential that ordinary folks have to take charge of their communities when given half a chance. You can be the one who affords that chance. Sometimes, while working with residents on a plan, you will need to be in the forefront (e.g., presenting or explaining complicated data). Sometimes, you need only facilitate their action (e.g., offer a structured process for goal setting). At other times, you need to sit quietly at the back and bite your tongue (e.g., when they are considering what is good and bad about their neighborhood).

One of the forms the professional-citizen relationship may take occurs when citizens undertake neighborhood planning on their own, and later, after they have completed a fair amount of work and a draft document, a professional planner enters the picture to finalize their plan. In such situations, the professional planner faces a challenge of building on—without violating—what the residents have created. This can become touchy if the professional legitimately disagrees with the citizens' direction, or finds they neglected some critical data that would affect their decisions, or is under city hall pressure to move the plan in wildly different directions. The residents too face a challenge in accepting outside help where it will enhance what they have done, while guarding what they have done, without getting overprotective and closed minded about it. The do-it-yourself approach is advocated throughout this guide because of the skill development, sense of ownership, and sense of empowerment that it engenders, but it would be foolish to reject expertise that may help you reach goals. Throughout the guide, I will offer comments and suggestions where I think a point needs to be made about the relationship between professional and citizen planner or about tasks particularly suited to the professional.

Neighborhood planners often develop a close attachment to their neighborhoods, i.e., the ones with which they are working. The neighborhood setting may well offer an excitement and vitality that the downtown city planning office does not. Perhaps for this reason, younger planners are especially attracted to this field of planning. The field may, however, be a minefield, strewn with professional and political dangers not immediately visible. Chief among them is the issue of *allegiance* should the neighborhood and the planning office or city administration have differing views of the world. What is the planner to do in such circumstances? One option, of course, is to declare your allegiance—whether to the job or the residents—and prepare to take the consequences: possible loss of employment or of the residents' confidence.

However, those extreme positions are not usually necessary or advisable: there are other steps you can take. First of all, it would be wise for the planner not to personalize the situation by staying in the middle of the controversy. Instead, be sure the residents understand where and how to address their position and then back out. Difficult as this may be to believe, they probably do not really need you as a savior anyway! Second, be sure the neighborhood understands the situation, namely, the planner is not the planning director or the mayor, and thus cannot make some things happen that they would like to see happen. Third, be sure the neighborhood's position has been conveyed to city officials as clearly and neutrally as possible. Fourth, there are perhaps others who should be in the middle of the fray, instead of the planner, such as the neighborhood's council member, who was elected to be in that politicized position, and has more power to bring about resolution than does the planner.

Now, such general guidelines are certainly subject to modification based on the particulars of the situation, the neighborhood, and the community. I have, for instance, known at least one planner who declared allegiance to the neighborhood and took his lumps for it. But he carefully (I believe) decided on that moral posture and knew what lay ahead. This little foray into the realm of conflict should suggest to the reader that this process you are about to embark on is not all peaches and cream. Head into it with your eyes open!

Let me suggest that the user of this guide start that adventure by reading through the entire guide rather than yielding to the temptation to flip to and start at one section that may attract. I have tried to organize the sequence of sections in the order you are likely to need them. Chapter 1 will introduce you to what planning is all about, including a few notions the professional planner may not have encountered before. Chapter 2 goes through the steps of planning, particularly emphasizing ways to make the process democratic and participatory. In Chapter 3, I cover the substance of the plan: what information will be needed, where and how to obtain it, and how to put it together. Chapter 4 discusses implementation of the plan.

One of the assumptions guiding the preparation of this guide was that it would be a group of people who would be thinking about doing a neighborhood plan. Reading the final portion of Chapter 2 should make it clear that it takes a fair amount of energy over a sustained period of time to crank out such a plan. If the professional planner envisions launching a neighborhood planning project with just a few interested citizens, or if it is just one or two citizens who are revved up to do a plan without a planner, I commend you. However, I also suggest in the strongest possible terms that you immediately set about the task of expanding your base before you go any farther. Reading the whole guide might be useful as a first step, so that you can convey more clearly to folks what it is you are trying to rope them into doing. Chapter 2 also gives a quick overview of the steps normally involved in doing a neighborhood plan, which are then fleshed out in Chapters 3 and 4.

No less than planning itself, writing about planning should be an organic process. Therefore, I welcome your feedback about this guide and what experiences (positive and negative) you have using it. Only by hearing from you, can I improve future editions of the guide.

Good luck!

An Introduction to Neighborhood Planning

THE CITY'S PLANNING PROCESS

Reasons for Planning

Planning is nothing more than systematically thinking through a situation in order to come up with a better decision. In our everyday lives, each of us engages in various instances of planning: deciding how we need to look as we select our clothes, determining how to avoid a rush-hour traffic jam, selecting where to take a vacation, or calculating how to be financially ready for retirement. A city, being far more complex than any one of us, also needs to engage in planning so that it can accommodate the needs and wishes of its residents for housing, schools, parks, roads, stores, offices, social services, garbage collection, water, and so on. Planners work not only in city planning offices, but in public works, parks and recreation, budgeting, social service, and other city hall agencies.

Planning has become a basic city function in all but the smallest communities.[1] Those of you who have been professional planners for any length of time have undoubtedly seen your ranks grow as planning has become a taken-for-granted activity in our cities. Planning is needed (at least) on the basis of order, empowerment, economy, and the environment.

Planning goes on all the time in our cities as individual persons, institutions, corporations, and governments make decisions. Many of those decisions (to put a new awning on my storefront, to resod my lawn, to change the route of the garbage truck) are small and do not add up to much. Others are larger ones: closing a store, building a new school, changing the street pattern. If these kinds of decisions are not coordinated, even though they may meet the needs of the party making the decision, they may not be in the general public interest. The world is made up of interconnected people, places, and spaces, and the actions of one affect others. Thus, in an effort to bring some *order* into the world, we plan.

Increasingly in our society, there are entities whose decisions are anything but small. A decision by a real estate developer to construct a 300-unit residential complex can radically alter a neighborhood, as can the decision by a school board to close down the elementary school, or the decision of a multinational corporation to close/open/expand a factory near your neighborhood. If residents are to have any impact on their surroundings, they need to develop a plan for its future, rather than trusting that their interests will be taken into account and protected by those various large decisionmakers. If residents wish to be *empowered*, they need to act in the systematic fashion that characterizes planning.

Planning can pave the way for the most efficient use of the scarce resources of our cities. Through planning, we can identify the highest priorities to which we'll direct our resources. We can devise alternative, and maybe less costly, ways to address some problem. We can mount projects that meet several needs at once, thus "killing two birds with one stone." We can pinpoint purchases that can be made at today's lower prices to meet future needs. In other words, planning can bring a measure of *economy* to public decisionmaking.

Finally, our fragile *environment* demands that we plan. Natural resources are not so inexhaustible that we can afford to be wasteful with land, water, or clean air. And the natural environment is not so resilient that we can disregard how human activities affect the land, the water, and the air.

So, for all those and probably many other reasons, cities engage in planning. My defense of planning should not be taken as a defense for those who would abuse and have abused planning by doing it in an elitist way, a way that excludes citizens from participation, a way that is secretive, or a way that uses planning as a way to oppress people. This kind of planning does go on and is to be condemned. But its existence should not be used to condemn all planning.

Kinds of City Plans

City planners (either hired staff or consultants retained by the city) prepare various forms of plans. First is the *comprehensive* or *master plan*, which is a broad brushstroke kind of plan. It usually takes the form of a series of interrelated policy statements, with some maps showing areas of generally preferred uses. The comp plan will address such topics as land use, housing, transportation, economy, culture, utilities, services, parks, and neighborhoods. What the comp plan says about neighborhoods will generally be at a rather general level, because the city's neighborhoods are all so different.

A second kind of plan some cities draft is a more detailed plan for some *functional area*, such as housing, human services, capital improvements, or for some city-owned facility, such as parks or health facilities. In fact, to qualify for certain federal housing programs, a city will often be required to complete a housing assistance plan. This kind of plan may make reference to specific neighborhoods, where a certain kind of public action is needed, such as housing rehabilitation or storm sewer construction.

Increasingly cities are engaging in *social planning*, to address such issues as homelessness, hunger, cultural arts, and the like. Again, references to neighborhoods in this third type of plan will either be very general or aimed at a few specific neighborhoods.

Fourth, cities engage in small area or *subarea planning*, which means a plan for some area less than the entire city. Two chief examples are plans for downtown areas and neighborhood plans.

So, the neighborhood plan, though a relatively recent arrival on the scene, is nothing very different than the other varieties of plans cities produce. It just deals with a smaller geographic area and rounds out the picture of what forms of planning are needed: from the comprehensive plan to the neighborhood plan, from the physical plan to the social plan.

THE CITYWIDE NEIGHBORHOOD
CONSERVATION PLAN

The Need

Rare is the city that has a *citywide* plan for the conservation of neighborhoods, although they may have conservation plans for particular neighborhoods and a citywide comprehensive plan. A citywide neighborhood conservation plan is something different. Such a plan is needed for a number of reasons. It provides a framework within which each specific neighborhood plan fits. The citywide neighborhood conservation plan identifies the different neighborhoods and categorizes them. It recognizes the individuality of each neighborhood in the city and its value as part of the mosaic that is the city. Looking at the city as a mosaic, a citywide neighborhood conservation plan states how neighborhoods relate to each other and to citywide uses and areas.

Any neighborhood in a city faces some issue that warrants conservation efforts to be sure the neighborhood does not start to decline. When neighborhood decline occurs, those problems sometimes spill over to adjacent neighborhoods. Thus, neighborhoods whose problems are left unattended may adversely affect adjacent areas. Public officials need to know how the problems in a given area and actions proposed for that area or requests made by that neighborhood might affect other neighborhoods. The identification of the neighborhood mosaic in a citywide neighborhood conservation plan, therefore, can represent a very valuable document. Why we do not see more such plans is anyone's guess. One city that does have a citywide neighborhood conservation plan is Cheyenne, Wyoming, and some of this section is based on that plan.

Contents

A citywide neighborhood conservation plan is different from the comprehensive plan or separate neighborhood plan. It is at a finer scale (i.e., more detailed) than a normal comprehensive plan; it focuses strictly on the issue of livability; it doesn't address some citywide or central business district issues. A comprehensive plan is at a broad brushstroke policy level and identifies areas for general types of uses. It does not usually say much about neighborhoods except at a very general level. The contents of a citywide neighborhood conservation plan would include:

1. definition of each neighborhood and its agreed-on boundaries.
2. identification, for each neighborhood, of what should be . . .
   preserved
   added
   removed
   kept out.
3. identification of the agents (implementers) of conservation and their respective tasks.
4. identification of conservation tasks by types of neighborhoods (neighborhoods can be categorized by the type of conservation work they require).

5. steps for implementation.

6. process for evaluation of the plan.

If such a plan is available for a city, the task of doing specific neighborhood plans is then greatly eased because some of the necessary analysis and thinking about needed actions has already been accomplished. Conversely, as a separate neighborhood plan is finished, it provides useful information to help modify the citywide neighborhood conservation plan.

Agents of Neighborhood Conservation

The key agents of conservation are neighborhood organizations, public officials, and developers; others might include schools, businesses, and social agencies. Identifying these parties as agents of neighborhood conservation is not to say that they always act in the best interests of neighborhoods.

Neighborhood organizations act as a stabilizing force in a neighborhood by bringing people together to address problems. Those organizations provide a repository or memory of what has gone on so the cumulative impacts of many small changes made over time can be detected. Neighborhood organizations offer a forum where pressing issues can be discussed. They give an identifiable spokesperson or contact point for those outside the neighborhood. Organizations tend to be more thoughtful than individual residents. Finally, once they are recognized and seen as legitimate, such organizations tend to act even more reasonably. Some planning officials may read this with great doubt, and, based on some past experiences, that doubt may be justified. The point being made here is that when neighborhood organizations are looked on as a full partner in the planning process, they do act as responsibly as any other entity in the city.

Public officials constitute agents of neighborhood conservation, because they are charged with looking at the larger picture of what occurs in a city even as many small changes go on within various sections of the city. Their role is to state publicly accepted principles, based on constituents' values, and make decisions. They bring technical expertise to the neighborhood. Last, they represent the citywide institutional memory. Some citizens reading this may react with skepticism as well! Again, start with a positive picture of the city officials and hold their feet to the fire should they veer away from their responsibilities toward the city's neighborhoods.

Developers can be agents of neighborhood conservation because they are bearers of resources to provide things the neighborhood may need, thus increasing the area's economic base. They trigger change in a neighborhood by forcing a healthy questioning of what has been taken for granted.

Other agents of neighborhood conservation, such as schools, businesses, and social agencies, by the resources they possess and the services they offer, help create the quality of life of a neighborhood.

THE NATURE OF A NEIGHBORHOOD PLAN

Neighborhood plans are sets of recommendations about how to improve a given area of a city. They are based on an analysis of a large amount of data collected about that area and generally represent the consensus among those stakeholders (residents and others) who have participated in drafting the plan. A professional planner, employed by the city, usually guides a neighborhood through the preparation of its plan, but as we are now seeing, residents often do the job on their own. The plan's recommendations are usually in two forms: *written statements* about some actions that should be taken and *maps* of the conditions the plan is designed to achieve. Just because a plan has been drafted, however, does not guarantee that any of the recommendations will be implemented: its contents are just that—recommendations. (Later parts of this guide will discuss how plans tend to get implemented.)

In most cities, there is a master or comprehensive plan to guide overall development of the city. Neighborhood plans are usually drafted in such a way as to be consistent (or at least not inconsistent) with the comprehensive plan and are often officially adopted as amendments to the comp plan. It is also possible to reverse that process, first drafting the neighborhood plans, and then combining them together into the comp plan. However, this approach is not the one usually taken.

REASONS FOR DOING A
NEIGHBORHOOD PLAN

Neighborhood plans are usually completed for a number of interrelated reasons. Such documents provide a guide for future development of the area since, if prepared correctly, they represent articulated shared visions about the future. At the same time, they identify tasks that need to be carried out to improve the area. Neighborhood plans get implemented, in fact, only if residents, with assistance from their neighborhood planner, systematically work to get the plan's recommendations acted on by the appropriate parties. Because the plan's recommendations are based on information systematically collected, they offer good support for positions that the neighborhood may wish to take on specific proposed changes. When a project is proposed that is inconsistent with the neighborhood plan, pointing out that inconsistency to city council, the planning board, or whomever, gives some weight to the residents' argument. In addition, that information can be used to justify requests or proposals made to the city (or to other funding sources) for services or funds. Sometimes, in fact, a particular funding source will not grant a request unless there is a neighborhood plan in place. These are the usual intended uses of a neighborhood plan.

In addition, there are likely to be side benefits, depending on how the planning work is done. Those might include increased citizen involvement, the development of leadership among the residents, and an increase in knowledge about and commitment to the neighborhood. All these can be collectively referred to as *community development.* These side benefits come about only if the planning process has been one that actively involves residents. For a neighborhood without an existing organization, the drafting of a plan can be the genesis of an organization as residents come together for the first time, learn more about each other and their neighborhood, and start developing a common vision about what they want it to be like. Working with planning students a few years ago, I saw that happen as our team assembled residents in an area without any prior organization. By the end of the semester, there were the beginnings of a viable organization, which I am happy to say is still alive at last report.

Researchers William Rohe and Lauren Gates (1985) have shown that compared to traditional planning approaches, neighborhood planning programs generally are more responsive to local characteristics, desires, and problems; may get more people involved in planning activities; generally result in more physical improvements actually being made; help strengthen communities through the increased interaction for those people involved in the plan; help leaders become more involved in citywide affairs; often lead to a fairer distribution of public resources; and may increase citizen access to and trust of local government. Sounds almost like a magic elixir, does it not? Note the qualifiers such as "generally" and "may." Still, neighborhood planning brings local government closer to people, if people insist on it and take advantage of it! That is a two-way street: the city has to take steps to foster neighborhood planning, and residents have to decide to participate.

DEFINING YOUR NEIGHBORHOOD

Importance

A study I did a number of years ago in Denver showed that virtually every major agency in city hall carved up the city into various service areas for its own administrative purposes. That seems a reasonable action for program managers to take. Strangely, none of the lines they drew on maps coincided with the actual neighborhoods in the city! New York City has actually gone a long way toward getting their administrators' lines to concur with the lines neighborhood organizations draw.

One of the first things a neighborhood and the local neighborhood planner have to do when embarking on a planning project is agree on what the neighborhood boundaries are. Usually this is neither very complicated nor controversial: many neighborhoods are conveniently bound by major barriers or edges, such as railroad tracks, highways, parks, rivers, and the like. Or perhaps the neighborhood has been defined as one newly developed, free-standing subdivision. Everyone then pretty much understands where the neighborhood is. Other times, there is controversy when residents of one area do not want to include some other blocks in their neighborhood, or when several associations all claim the same turf.

Some city planning departments have divided their entire city into neighborhoods on the basis of census tracts, the ones used in the federal census every ten years. This is very convenient in that the planning department can then track changes from 1970 to 1980 to 1990 because those lines rarely are changed. But those lines may have nothing to do with the way people define where they live. It is important that residents make others understand what the boundaries of the neighborhood are, as they see them. Planners are well advised not to assume the lines you may have drawn on a map at the office will automatically be accepted out on the street.

Methods

A number of different methods can be used to determine systematically what the residents call their boundaries if there is no agreement at the outset of a planning project. Those who show up at the initial meetings can simply declare what the boundaries are; that is probably the simplest, but not necessarily the best or fairest method.

Different types of surveys can be done. A representative sample of residents can be asked, for instance, to draw lines on maps. When all the maps are put together, some lines will stand out as most agreed on. Residents can also be asked a lengthy set of questions about how they use the neighborhood: where they walk or do not walk, where they drive or do not drive, where they shop for various items, what park they use, and so on. Small businesses can be asked about the area from which they draw their customers. Observers walking and driving the neighborhood can map out where things (e.g., housing styles or lifestyles) start to change. When all those pieces of information are plotted on maps, one starts to get some sense of the common area that means something to people.

A neighborhood entering into a planning process should not have to conduct a major research project just to decide what it is they are planning. However, it is advisable at least to have some decent discussion about the matter rather than having just a few leaders or someone from outside the neighborhood arbitrarily decide what your neighborhood is.

Notes

1. The frame of reference for this guide is the city and the neighborhoods within it, but, of course, suburban areas also have neighborhoods and do their own version of neighborhood planning. In fact, the newness of some suburbs appears to make them even more amenable to involving citizens in planning projects.

2. Gary Long, Bernie Jones, Paul Foster, Paul Heath, Roy Fronczyk. 1984. *Cheyenne Neighborhood Conservation Plan.* Report prepared for the Cheyenne-Larimer County Planning Commission.

2

Democratic Neighborhood Planning

PRINCIPLES OF NEIGHBORHOOD PARTICIPATION

The Four Ds

The assumption is often made that neighborhood planning will be done democratically, but that is not always the case. It sometimes happens that (a) a neighborhood plan is prepared by city staff or a consultant with only minimal contact and involvement of the residents or (b) a plan is prepared by some residents—a small band of self-selected ones—who do not bother to involve any of their neighbors.

One way of thinking about democratic neighborhood planning is to think of four Ds:

- **deprofessionalization**—it is not just professionals shaping the future of the neighborhood
- **decentralization**—the decisionmaking is not concentrated downtown
- **demystification**—the magic is taken out of planning—it becomes user-friendly, if you will
- **democratization**—more people are involved directly in decisionmaking, especially those with a stake (stakeholders) in the neighborhood's future.

Philosophers and political figures over the years have argued about the

11

nature and desirability of democracy. For purposes of neighborhood planning, democratic participation is important for three key reasons.

1. The greater the participation of residents in the making of a plan, the more likely it is that the plan will accurately reflect their needs and concerns.
2. The greater the participation, the greater is the sense of ownership that people have about the plan, which can translate into a greater determination on their part to see that the plan gets implemented.
3. The greater the participation, the harder it is for others, such as public officials, to ignore the plan.

Real Participation

It should be noted that just doing some research on how people use the neighborhood or on what their concerns are by itself is not democratic participation. That is what academics call *user needs research*, that is, research about the needs of users, and that is not the same thing as active involvement in the planning. Also, merely getting citizen input is not full democratic participation. Again, that is just getting information from people, not necessarily actively involving them in planning. The question one has to ask about both of these forms of planning is "Who gets to use the information to create a plan?"

The distinction being hammered away at here is between a passive role as an information source and an active role as a citizen-planner. A group of residents doing a neighborhood plan on their own can fall into the trap of using their fellow residents simply as passive information sources, just as a city planner can fall into the trap of thinking that merely getting input is real citizen participation. Doing things democratically takes more effort and more time, but it is worth it for the quality of product that emerges and the sense of commitment that people will have toward it. One neighborhood planner I know notes that democracy is based on the conviction "that there are extraordinary possibilities in ordinary people." It is the responsibility of those organizing the planning, whether residents or staff, to be sure that everyone has been afforded the chance for active participation.

General Guidelines

There are some general guidelines that can assist democratic neighborhood planning, whether carried out by a professional planner or by citizens on their own. First, people need to be involved from the very beginning before the crucial decisions that frame everything else are made.

Second, the flowchart is one of the first things that should be settled; that diagram of the planning process tells who does what, when, what the roles are, and how each parties' contribution is related to the overall process. Figure 2–1 lists the seven steps used and shows on a Gantt chart when they would be completed. Figure 2–2 shows more specifically the roles to be played by the planners and by the residents. A flowchart for a neighborhood-initiated planning process might look somewhat different, but the principle is the same: spell out the steps and the responsibilities.

Figure 2-1. Planning Process Flowchart A

Activities	Sept. 22	29	Oct. 6	13	20	27	Nov. 3	10	17	24	Dec. 1	8
Data collection and analysis	X	X	X									
Issue identification		X	X									
Community goal setting			X	X								
Concept development				X	X	X						
Alternatives generation and selection						X	X	X	X			
Final recommendation									X	X	X	X
Presentation											X	X

Third, do not assume several residents who came together when you called a meeting to start a neighborhood plan is a group. They may well come from very disparate backgrounds or may have little experience working in groups. It may be necessary to spend time at initial meetings doing things just to solidify the group. Group-building techniques might range from informal events like potluck suppers to more formal exercises, like those suggested by Cyril Mills in *Activities for Trainers: 50 Useful Designs*. In addition, it should not be assumed that everyone in the neighborhood is pursuing the same goals. Neighbors may have opposing or hidden agendas. To the extent that efforts are made at the front end to create a sense of group identity, there is a greater chance for these competing agendas to be aired and maybe even resolved.

Figure 2-2. Planning Process Flowchart B

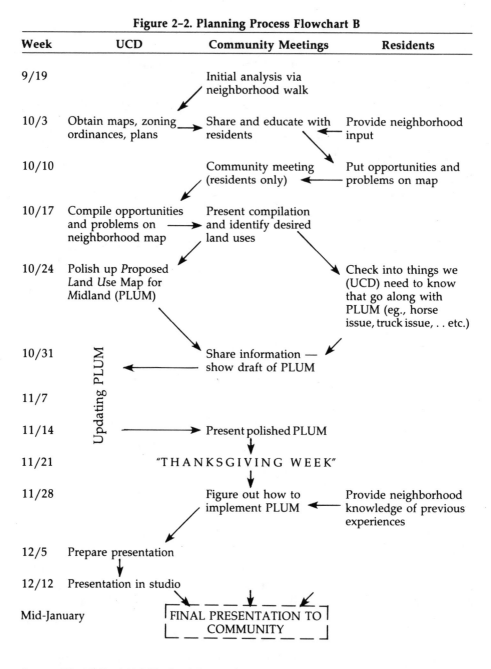

Week	UCD	Community Meetings	Residents
9/19		Initial analysis via neighborhood walk	
10/3	Obtain maps, zoning ordinances, plans	Share and educate with residents	Provide neighborhood input
10/10		Community meeting (residents only)	Put opportunities and problems on map
10/17	Compile opportunities and problems on neighborhood map	Present compilation and identify desired land uses	
10/24	Polish up *Proposed Land Use* Map for Midland (PLUM)		Check into things we (UCD) need to know that go along with PLUM (eg., horse issue, truck issue, . . etc.)
10/31	Updating PLUM	Share information — show draft of PLUM	
11/7			
11/14		Present polished PLUM	
11/21		"THANKSGIVING WEEK"	
11/28		Figure out how to implement PLUM	Provide neighborhood knowledge of previous experiences
12/5	Prepare presentation		
12/12	Presentation in studio		
Mid-January		FINAL PRESENTATION TO COMMUNITY	

Source: *The Midland Neighborhood Proposed Land Use Plan,* 1984, by the University of Colorado at Denver, Center for Community Development and Design.

Fourth, remind everyone at each stage of the work what has been accomplished thus far and what the next steps are. That not only reinforces people for what they have accomplished but it gives them an idea of where things are headed. This is a task for the professional, if there is one involved. One easy way to keep a picture of the whole process in mind is to make sure everyone has a looseleaf binder, with tabs, in which they can keep all the materials generated accessible and easy to locate.

Fifth, offer residents a smorgasbord of ways to get involved so there is no excuse for not getting involved. Some people do not like going to public meetings, so offer them a questionnaire or something else. Those who do not like a questionnaire might be willing to drop by an open house. The planning team and the professional planner have to accept the responsibility for making it easy for people to become involved. You cannot just hang out your shingle, expect people to show up, and criticize them when they do not. Find out what avenues of involvement they prefer and offer them a number of different ways to get involved.

Sixth, do not utilize the assumption that laypeople cannot understand some things: "Oh, it's just some technical information you do not need to bother with." Residents need to insist that technical information be made understandable, or it may be used against them, while professionals need to make it available.

Seventh, at critical junctures during the process and definitely at the end, do not forget to celebrate. Celebration reaffirms your sense of who you all are and what you have accomplished together.

ALTERNATIVE METHODS OF
PARTICIPATION

There are a number of different approaches to involving neighbors in the planning process. Some are actually best seen as outreach methods (that is, just getting the word out that planning is going on); some are methods for gathering data about people and the neighborhood; and some are methods by which people actually participate in planning work. For democratic neighborhood planning to occur, all are needed, but the first two methods, without the third, will not give you real democratic participation.

Outreach Methods

Personal Contact. Included under personal contact are door-to-door visits and phone calling. In many ways, these are the best outreach methods because they are the most personalized. However, they can be time-consuming. One way to cut short the time required is to organize a phone tree, where one person calls three other people, who each call five other people and so on. The door knocking work usually includes leaving a flyer or leaflet describing the planning project and announcing the next meeting (see Figure 2–3).

Media. The local electronic and print media can help your planning team do its outreach work. Most radio stations and newspapers, and some TV stations, will run your press release or public service announcement (PSA) if you get it to them in proper time and form (see Figure 2-4). Ask them, and they will gladly tell you their guidelines. If your community has a public service cable channel, you are sure to have ample opportunity to plug your project. As a last resort, space can be purchased in the print or electronic media, but that is usually not necessary.

Field Office/Drop-in Center. What is involved here is having a physical place, such as retail store front, where residents can drop in and learn about the neighborhood planning process. Typically, there are maps, photographs, flowcharts of the process, and other visual displays. Ideally, such a place is staffed with someone who can answer questions and give out information. There can also be the opportunity to gather data, using questionnaires that visitors are asked to complete. This site should be in a high traffic, high visibility area, such as a popular retail center. Offering the planning team free or cheap use of the space could be a nice way for a neighborhood merchant or property owner to make a contribution to the planning project.

Utilize Existing Organizations. The meetings, offices, or newsletters of existing organizations can be very helpful channels of communication for letting residents know of the planning process. At meetings, personal presentations can be made, especially by participants, who like those attending, are from the neighborhood. For newsletters, a short article can be prepared, or if the organization will allow, a flyer (especially on bright-colored paper) inserted into the newsletter. Flyers and posters can be displayed at the offices of these organizations. Certainly other neighborhood institutions—churches, supermarkets, community centers, post offices, and so on—can be similarly used for getting the word out.

Figure 2–3. Leaflet

COMMUNITY MEETING!

Wednesday, December 3, 7:30 p.m.
East High School Main Entrance on 16th

The Colfax at the Park project is a community-based effort to improve East Colfax from York to Colorado Blvd. This project is using the combined efforts of neighborhood residents, local businesspeople, and a planning team from the University of Colorado at Denver.

The December 3 meeting, third in a fall series, will focus on strategies that the Colfax at the Park community can use to *positively* affect the future of this area. Attend this meeting to help both Colfax's future, and the future of your neighborhood.

An example of possible work on the 3200 block south

Sponsored By South City Park,
Congress Park Neighbors,
and Capitol Hill United Neighborhoods

Figure 2–4. Public Service Announcement

Greater Delmar Neighbors
3415 W. Fortune St.
Denver, CO 80223
(303) 495-0932

Public Service Announcement

For Immediate Use
After Feb. 15, 1990;
Use Through March 6

Contact:
Yolanda Stillwell
645-2670

Greater Delmar Neighbors and the city's planning office will kick off a neighborhood planning project with a community meeting Tuesday, March 6 at 7 p.m., at Delmar Middle School, 34th and Eudora. Residents and business people in the area between West 27th and West 43rd Streets, Archer to Mountain Streets are urged to attend to help decide the future of their neighborhood. For more information, call Yolanda Stillwell at the planning office, 645-2670.

Displays at Key Settings. Somewhat more elaborate than a flyer or poster tacked up somewhere would be a display about the planning process that might include such things as written information, photos, or maps. This could be in a very prominent place where many paths cross and could be changed periodically as the project moves along. If there is some site in the neighborhood that is central to the original need for a plan, such as a vacant lot, right in front of that might be the ideal place to plant the display (assuming it is a busy enough site).

Data-Gathering Methods

Responsive Publication. This device, which is used both for outreach and for data gathering, is something like a questionnaire, but it is slightly different. Basically, it is a printed page or two, with information about some issue, presented in a neutral fashion, which then also allows the person receiving it to register some opinion about the issue. So, it presents information and it asks some questions. The information could be about some particular aspect of the neighborhoods. During the course of the planning, a number of these might be issued, each on a different subject. The questions are usually limited (e.g., "Which of the three alternatives do you favor?" or "Do you support or oppose this?"). The responsive publication could also be printed in the local newspaper as a paid ad, or for free if the editor will permit.

Individual Interviews. The face-to-face interview will always be among the best ways to obtain information from individual people in a community. However, to be effective, it must be done well, and that entails preparing a good set of questions (the interview schedule), training interviewers, and selecting a large and representative sample. The neighbor-to-neighbor contact involved here is a real side benefit to interviewing.

Informal Consultation. Informal consultation means making casual contact with residents without having a predetermined set of questions shape the conversation. In fact, the contact is more of a conversation than an interview. This method might be more appropriate near the start of a planning process, when specific issues have not yet been identified, and you are just trying to get a general sense of how people see their neighborhood.

Direct Observation. Yogi Berra is reported to have said, "You can see a lot by looking." Direct observation is just a fancy name for looking, but doing it in a more disciplined or systematic way. Participants in a planning process might each be given a standard, preprinted form to use on which they would record how each property is being used, its physical conditions, and how people use the public spaces. To do this right requires a short training session, but it can then produce a wealth of data very quickly. If the analysis is all done at once, it can be followed by a party to raise community spirit(s).

With the wide availability of video tape recorders now, especially lightweight ones, there is a marvelous opportunity to produce simple tapes of the neighborhood. Great expertise is no longer required to operate such equipment. Group viewing of the tapes could stimulate very helpful (and likely entertaining) conversation.

Activity Log. In the context of neighborhood planning, an activity log would be a record of activities a person did outdoors in public. Typically, a person, who agrees to cooperate, is given a simple form (see Figure 2–5) on which to record activities every 15 minutes for a few days. When a large number of these are collected and analyzed, patterns of use in the neighborhood will likely stand out clearly.

Figure 2–5. Activity Log

Time	What were you doing? How long did it take?	Who, if anybody, was with you?	Where did you do it?	Is this a typical activity for you?
6:00 a.m.				
6:15 a.m.				
6:30 a.m.				
6:45 a.m.				
7:00 a.m.				
7:15 a.m.				
7:30 a.m.				
7:45 a.m.				
etc.				

Behavioral Mapping. This technique of making systematic observations about how people are using a particular space within the neighborhood is for learning more about specific, small areas, not the neighborhood as a whole. Examples of spaces the planning group might wish to observe in this way would be a small neighborhood park, an open space near a school, a busy neighborhood-oriented retail center. Since this technique can be very time-consuming, you will probably want to reserve use of it for some few spaces that are especially problematic.

Very concrete categories of behavior are first identified; examples might be walking, playing, sitting, or reading, or even deviant acts such as drug-dealing. (Be careful here: your job is not to engage in dangerous vigilanteeism, but to understand the neighborhood!) Other information would also be collected, such as characteristics of the persons being observed (approximate age, sex, ethnic background, or observations about whether the person is alone, in a couple, or part of a larger group). Observations then have to be made over some time—say several weeks, at various times of day, on different days, in order to have a good sample of observations. Data of this sort are then charted on maps, so that patterns of heavy or light use, or of certain kinds of uses start to emerge (see Figures 2–6 and 2–7).

Figure 2-6. Behavioral Map A

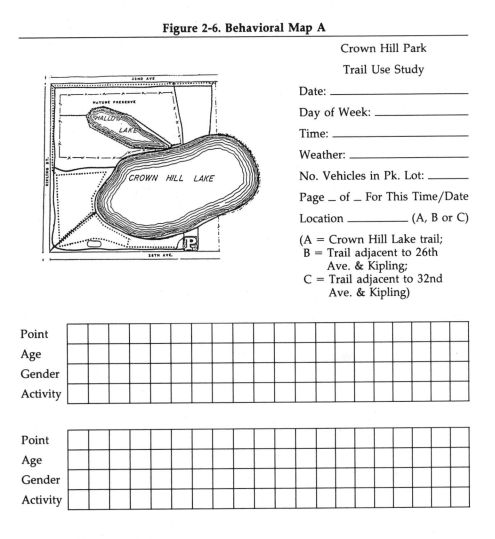

Crown Hill Park

Trail Use Study

Date: _____

Day of Week: _____

Time: _____

Weather: _____

No. Vehicles in Pk. Lot: _____

Page _ of _ For This Time/Date

Location _____ (A, B or C)

(A = Crown Hill Lake trail;
B = Trail adjacent to 26th
  Ave. & Kipling;
C = Trail adjacent to 32nd
  Ave. & Kipling)

Point																					
Age																					
Gender																					
Activity																					

Point																					
Age																					
Gender																					
Activity																					

Comments/Observed Conflicts:

Activity: A = pedestrian; B = bicycle; C = runner; D = disabled; E = equestrian;
F = fisherman; G = fitness trail user; H = skater/skateboard; J = pic-
nicker/stationary person; P = pet on leash; S = baby stroller

Source: *Crown Hill Park Visitor Profiles and Management Recommendations* 1987, by William R.
Haase. University of Colorado at Denver, Center
for Built Environment Studies.

Figure 2-7. Behavioral Map B

SETTING: _Brent Park playground_
NUMBER OF OBSERVATIONS _6_
TIME COVERED: _July 6-22_

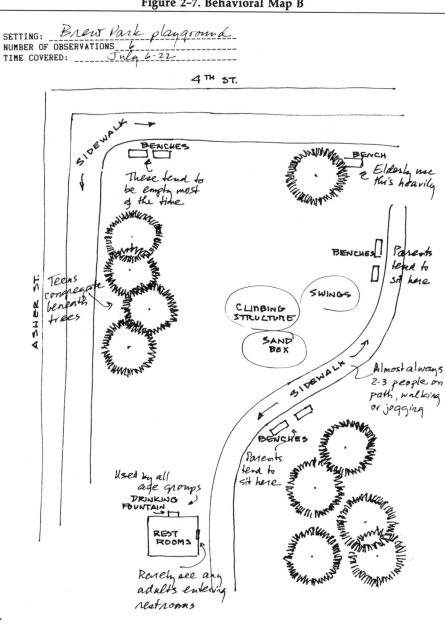

Advisory Committee/Reactor Panel. This method entails creating a small, select group of residents who are contacted every so often, shown the work that has been done to date, and asked for a reaction. (This method is more likely to be utilized by an outsider doing a plan for a neighborhood, rather than by residents themselves; it is included here so the reader is aware of yet one more technique.)

Walking Tour. A nice way to get people together, get them doing something active, and also generate useful information is to arrange a walking tour. This is nothing more than a small group of people walking through the neighborhood together, talking about it as they go. (Depending on the size of the area, some part of the tour might be by bus or van.) The planner, walking with them, may toss out questions ("What do you think of those stores over there?," or "Are there usually so few people in that park?") to spur on conversation. Carrying a small tape recorder and recording the conversation helps retain more of what was said. Perhaps some photos could be taken as reminders of features many people discussed. Gathering back at the school, church basement, or someone's house after the walk affords an opportunity to structure the conversation more, synthesize it, and socialize.

Surveys. The time-honored method of gathering information from a group of people is to prepare a questionnaire and then distribute it very widely throughout the community. Surveying can allow a planning group to gather information about a large number of issues from a large number of people. Preparing a bad questionnaire, however, is very easy, while preparing a good one takes some effort and skill. In addition, care must be exercised in drawing up a sample to be sure it is representative of the neighborhood. Assuming these barriers can be overcome, the survey is a great tool, producing masses of data that are nicely quantifiable. Many people can be involved in the survey by playing roles in suggesting questions, in distributing and picking up the questionnaires, and in tabulating results. A sample questionnaire can be found in Appendix B.

Several different methods are available for getting the questionnaires out: mailing them, hand-delivering them, having people pick them up at various locations, and printing them in the newspaper. They can be returned by mail, hand collected, or dropped off at central locations. One of the best ways to assure a good response rate is by dropping them off at homes, securing a commitment from somebody who's there that it will be filled out, and then returning 24 hours later (or even 4 to 5 hours later) to collect them. The sample questionnaire in Appendix B, originally used in a small town, has some useful ideas for questions. The bibliography at the end of this guide lists some useful guides that provide more detailed guidance for groups considering doing a formal survey.

Participation Methods

Large Community Meetings. This is the method used most often in neighborhood planning to get participation from residents: you prepare an agenda, you reserve the school gym or the church basement, you distribute leaflets in the neighborhood, you prepare pots of coffee and donuts, and you wait, hope, and pray people show up! Done well, the general community meeting is very valuable; done poorly, it turns people off and they do not come back. Doing it well entails all those steps: preparing a nicely paced, engaging meeting, making sure you have used every conceivable channel of communication to get the word out, obtaining the use of and arranging a proper place, and having a few refreshments available.

Small Living Room Meetings. Known by some as the coffee klatsch, this type of meeting occurs at someone's home, with invitations usually being issued just to residents of the immediate block or other small area. It can be a very useful method in the early stages of a planning process. Its more intimate setting is usually less threatening and offers attendees more opportunity to interact informally. The planner might utilize this approach early on to broaden the base of participation, before getting into substantial work. (Once a planning process is under way, committees may meet in this fashion.)

Open House. The open house is a participation technique that might be combined with the field office/drop-in center. It is the creation of a special occasion when neighbors are invited to drop in and view such things as plans, data, and maps. This can be done even if there is not a regular field office: the open house can be held at a church, community center, business, or whatever space is available. It should be well advertised, limited to about four hours, and be held at a time thought appropriate for the neighborhood, such as an evening, or weekend afternoon. Refreshments and printed information should be available, as well as knowledgeable participants who can talk informally with visitors about the planning process going on. There should be some way attendees can register their views, such as on brief questionnaires, large newsprint tablets, or 3″ x 5″ index cards.

Workshops. This term covers a large variety of participation techniques. What is meant by the workshop essentially is an interactive meeting, where special techniques are used to stimulate participation and the flow of creative ideas. It may be done as a *charette*, which is a marathon-type session (e.g., all day Saturday, a full weekend, or three successive evenings). In the charette, there is usually the aim of completing some product, such as a draft plan, by the end of the session. Some expertise may be required to pull this off at least if some specialized techniques, such as those which follow, are going to be used. Generally, a neighborhood planner staging a charette will recruit other staff members to help out. Having the head of the planning office there, as well as some elected officials, lends an air of credibility to the event.

- **Brainstorming.** This is simply the process of asking people for their ideas and then encouraging a rapid-fire flow of ideas, without discussion, questioning, or challenging. All ideas are initially taken as legitimate and written down on large newsprint pads for later use.
- **Presenter, Panel, or Debate.** Having some people at the front of the audience who present some organized comments can be an effective way to generate ideas and subsequent participant discussion. This may be one speaker or a panel of residents or outside experts. They may each present their views or a moderator may oversee a debate.
- **Trial.** A variation of the above techniques would be to stage a mock trail, complete with an accused, a prosecutor, a defense attorney, and a jury. In the context of neighborhood planning, the charge might be that "the neighborhood is ugly." Someone then makes the charge, someone else defends, and the jury (maybe a few people or the whole audience) argues to a verdict. The trial illustrates the idea that imagination should be given free rein in the task of bringing people together to deliberate about their neighborhood.
- **Buzz Groups.** This is a fancy name for breaking a large group into small groups to discuss, brainstorm, devise alternative solutions, and so on. The importance of the small group is that it allows greater participation by all members. Buzz groups usually designate someone to report their conclusions back to the full group once reassembled.
- **Role Playing.** Although somewhat threatening to some people, role playing can be very useful to help people understand some different

perspectives by placing them into roles different than the ones they usually occupy. Having neighbors, for instance, role play a housing developer or planning commissioner can be eye opening.

- **Nominal Group Process.** As one technique for structuring group brainstorming and discussion, the nominal group technique is extremely efficient when conducted properly. An issue is identified, and everyone is given 3″ x 5″ index cards to write down ideas for about five minutes. The group leader then asks for the ideas to be read off, one idea at a time, going around the room. All non-duplicated ideas are recorded and numbered on a large newsprint pad. Brief questions (for clarification only) are then allowed. At that point, if priorities are wanted, each person is given more cards on which to record the numbers of their preferred items. Votes are then tallied, and voila, there are your priorities. Discussion can be built into the process at any point, and variations on the process can be made. The key things are the tight structure, the chance to write down items on the cards (less threatening than having to call them out), and the public recording of all items for later discussion and/or vote.

- **Swirling.** This method allows very active participation in creating clusters of associated ideas through swirling. In this process, participants write ideas (e.g., goals, priorities, solutions, or whatever is called for at that stage of the planning process) on large (at least 5″ x 8″) cards with sticky backs (or regular index cards with masking tape), stick them on a large wall, and then move them around (swirling) to create clusters of ideas that hang together. This is effective in getting people up and moving (which keeps them awake and attentive) and allows easy reforming of the clusters. This technique is also useful for ordering tasks to get something done: the group can keep rearranging the steps until they arrive at an agreed-on sequence.

- **'Rite and Roam and Read.** Somewhat akin to the swirling technique is this one in which people write ideas on sheets of newsprint pad and tape them on the wall. Everyone then roams around and reads everyone else's ideas. The neighborhood planner or group leader can then begin a discussion by asking for comments such as common themes or contrasting goals. If need be, the leader can go around and mark key ideas or words with a contrasting color magic marker, but generally the participants will have seen those commonalities themselves.

- **Mechanical Catalyst.** This term, for lack of a better one, is used to describe anything that a planner or group leader might use as a stimulator of discussion, such as a slide show, videotape, photographs, map, or model. If people are reluctant to talk, something like this can help trigger comments.

Beyond these conventional techniques, group leaders can devise any number of additional ones to suit the occasion; the only limit is their creativity. In workshops, however, it is critical that one carefully assess the situation and the likely attendees to see what techniques will be acceptable. While you may want to have people stretch themselves a bit, you do not want to make them uncomfortable or embarrass them in public. Group leaders should always be ready to switch gears if the game plan is not working as expected: it is better to admit that to a group than to force through a process that is obviously not working and is getting everyone uptight.

RUNNING EFFECTIVE COMMUNITY MEETINGS

Good Meetings

As mentioned earlier, the community meeting is so widely utilized in neighborhood planning that it deserves some special attention. The neighborhood meeting is valuable because it offers the chance for residents to come together and work on common issues. In the process, they will likely grow individually and as a community, will strengthen their identities as members of that given neighborhood, and will get some important business done. For the neighborhood planner, the meeting is the occasion where you see as much of the neighborhood together as you are ever likely to see. It is a great opportunity to advance the planning work. But do not blow it or you might lose a whole bunch of people all at once!

Good meetings are ones where people leave feeling satisfied and look forward to the next one, where the people who needed to be there were there and even arrived on time, where everyone stayed until the end, where clear-cut decisions were made, where feelings could be aired, and where conflict was dealt with rather than avoided without the group self-destructing, and where participants felt rewarded for their contributions.

Those individuals who conduct the meeting need to be clear on its purpose. Is it simply to put information out, to receive information, to create new ideas, to get people interacting and comfortable with one another, or to make decisions? All of those (and others) are legitimate reasons to have meetings, but each would call for a different format, physical arrangement, schedule, and so on.

Agenda

The second part of staging a successful meeting is preparing the agenda, which defines the group's charge, what it wants to get done, and the order of business. An agenda should be prepared ahead of time and made available to everyone (handed out and/or visibly displayed in large print). Then it is a good idea to ask for approval of the agenda ("Is there anything else anyone wants to put on the agenda?"). In addition to giving everyone ownership of the agenda, this gives the group leader the ability to use the agenda to rule out extraneous discussion that might occur later.

The agenda ought to state both the beginning and the ending time for the meeting: this acts as a self-disciplining device to prevent some people from running on at the mouth. Stating the proposed time allotment for each agenda item also helps frame the discussion. It can also help to state briefly on the agenda what is the expected action for each item (e.g., information item only, discussion, decision). Finally, think carefully about the sequence of items on the agenda. In general, it is best to move from least to most controversial. Important items need to be near the middle since some people invariably arrive late and some leave early (see Figure 2–8).

Publicity

Third on the list of tasks for conducting a successful meeting is getting the word out. A number of ideas about this have been mentioned earlier under outreach methods. The important thing is simply to be sure the word did get out to all residents.

Audience Analysis

Before people arrive and as they are arriving, the alert neighborhood planner and/or the group leader will take the time to do some *audience analysis*. Who's there? Are there many people you have not seen before, who will need some updating on the whole planning process? Is there a contingent of people you know oppose the plan, who need to be given a chance to express that? Are there some very elderly and frail people, who may be uncomfortable with the very active format you had planned to use, which calls for small groups to form, break up, and reform?

Figure 2–8. Community Meeting Agenda

July 12, 1989
7:00–9:00 p.m.

Agenda

Introductions	5 minutes
Review and acceptance of agenda	5
Overview of planning project (Bonnie Felson)	5
Progress to date (Jack Smedly)	10
Tonight's task: identifying issues exercise (Betty Younger)	60
Presentation on current zoning issue (Planning Office representative)	10
Discussion and possible action on that	15
Looking ahead to next steps (Bonnie)	10
Announcements	
Adjournment	

Note: Thanks to 8th grade home economics class for the refreshments tonight!

Physical Arrangements

The physical arrangements and props for a community meeting can make or break a meeting. Are there chairs, tables, a podium, chalkboard, or a place to tape up newsprint sheets? Are the entrances to the building clearly marked ("Enter here for neighborhood meeting")? Can you control the heating, lighting, air conditioning, and do you know where those controls are? Is there a need for a mike and do you have one that works? What about a slide projector and screen (and spare bulb)? Do you know where there is a working outlet for the coffee pot? What about parking and exterior lighting? Should you have hired a local teenager to provide child care? Whose responsibility is it to rearrange and clean up the place? There are a million little details, mostly common sense, but very easy to forget!

The other part of the physical arrangements concerns *seating arrangements*. The best seating arrangement depends on what kind of meeting you hope to have. There are several common arrangements, suited to different kinds of meetings (see Figure 2–9).

A cardinal rule in arranging meetings is "beware the janitors," because they invariably set up long rows of chairs, one in back of the other (Arrangement A), the dreariest of arrangements for anything but watching a movie! The secret is to get there early enough so you have the chance to rearrange things. Remember, though, that many people have a reluctance to sit in the front row, and that empty front row can make a meeting seem sparsely attended, even when there is a decent turnout. If, when you first arrive at the meeting room, you set up just one or two rows of chairs, and add others behind those rows as people arrive, you will in effect have forced early arrivals into the front rows and make it seem like the place is packed! This entails some monitoring to be sure you set up chairs when needed, always keeping a few empty chairs available.

Figure 2-9. Seating Arrangements

A.

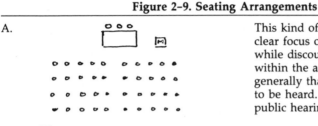

[M] = MICROPHONE

This kind of arrangement puts a clear focus on those at the front, while discouraging interaction within the audience. It requires generally that one go up to the front to be heard. This works fine for public hearings and forums.

[M = Microphone]

B. This also features a frontal focus, but allows better audience views of each other. Interaction is still discouraged, but at least one does not have to go to the front of the room to speak.

C. Much face-to-face interaction is certainly encouraged by this setup. Those at the ends of the tables will probably talk more and receive more attention. This is a poor arrangement if the table is very narrow.

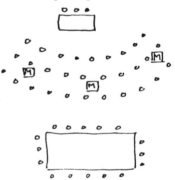

D.

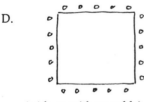

(with or without table)

With this arrangement, interaction is encouraged, but no one is cast in an obvious leader role. It may however put some people in a dead corner.

E. If space allows, you can use this arrangement to foster face-to-face interaction, and small group work or discussion. It is space-consuming, may be too diffuse, and tends to encourage side conversations, during general presentations.

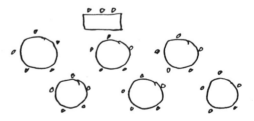

F. An alternative to the first two
    arrangements, this setup allows good
    interaction when a more
    conversational circle is not possible.
    A main speaker, of course, will have
    to do a bit of twisting and turning.

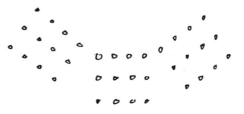

G.

A semicircle gives most of the
advantages of a circle when a circle
is not possible. Be sure to set up two
or four rows, or the odd middle row
will be left largely vacant.

H. The circle is probably the best
    all-around arrangement for
    community meetings because of the
    way it allows everyone to see
    everything, while also creating a
    very egalitarian atmosphere. If the
    space dictates, the circle can be
    refashioned into more of an oval.

Roles

There are a few key roles to be played by group leaders at community meetings, namely, the convener, the facilitator, and the scribe. The *convener* is the chairperson or president, or whoever will be running the meeting. This person must be seen as legitimate in the eyes of the attendees in order to be effective. He or she has the authority then to decide how to use the agenda to get the business done.

In the early phases of a neighborhood planning process, it may well be that the planner will need to chair the meetings, until sufficient leadership develops from among the residents (assuming there is not yet a viable neighborhood organization). Of course, this responsibility should then be turned over to the residents as soon as possible. A planner and a resident working in tandem is another possible arrangement. Still one other way to run the meeting is for a resident to be the overall convener, turning the meeting over to the planner for certain sections where the planner has more of the information needed for that phase of the meeting. What is most important is to make sure before the meeting that everyone has the same understanding of what is going to happen and who is going to do what, so that the meeting will flow smoothly.

Sometimes at a community meeting, it is helpful to have another person who is confident in using some of the techniques discussed earlier so as to manage the discussion. This is the *facilitator*, whose task it is to encourage the flow of discussion, yet keep it within the agreed-on bounds (of time and topic). This person is not a leader so much as a traffic cop, attending as much to the process of the discussion as to the content. The facilitator does not express his or her own views, but encourages others to do so, drawing out the silent, controlling the overly verbal, encouraging a healthy clash of ideas, and not letting anyone stomp on anyone else's ideas.

Again, the planner may fill the role of facilitator at some stages of work, such as early discussions of problems, issues, and overall goals. Later on, the planner might need to be more involved in the discussion than is appropriate for a facilitator.

In addition to the facilitator, it may be useful to have a *scribe*, that is, a public note taker. This person, armed with many colored magic markers, a fat pad of newsprint paper (at least 24″ x 36″), tape and/or push pins, makes a public record of the key points of the meeting. This public record also helps to stimulate conversation and serves as a group memory, as it were. The scribe's first qualification is being able to print clearly; other important challenges include listening closely and summarizing comments in a few words. Sometimes, the facilitator and the scribe are one and the same person. However, this can put an unreasonable burden on the person, so that having two people is preferred.

Any neighborhood planner can be expected to assume the scribe role at some meetings, and by virtue of professional training, should be equipped to fill the role. The planner in most circumstances would also be responsible for making sure all the needed supplies are on hand. Having a kit with markers, push pins, tape, etc. assembled is a must.

A parenthetical note is called for here: the planner whose professional education did not include preparation in these basic meeting skills was cheated. Some planning programs harbor the belief that map making, quantitative analysis, and theory will suffice. In neighborhood planning, people skills are equally important.

SELECTION OF PARTICIPATION METHOD

Out of all these various methods or techniques, how does a group of neighbors (or the neighborhood planner) doing a neighborhood plan select which ones to use? First of all, let it be said that there is probably no foolproof way to select the best one. Second, a combination of different methods is advised, using different ones at different stages of the planning process. In addition, different groups within the neighborhood might gravitate to different channels of communication and involvement.

Therefore, if you can offer a smorgasbord of opportunities, you are more likely to reach all groups. Third, one should be ready to switch approaches if the one selected is not working. Fourth, one should consider the nature of the community, the political situation, some practical considerations, and the nature of the project or task at hand. Following is a list of factors, categorized into those four areas, with an example in each case of how that factor might come into play.

FACTORS TO CONSIDER IN SELECTING METHODS FOR INVOLVING CITIZENS

Community Considerations:

Size—(behavioral mapping would be feasible in a small neighborhood, but not in large one).

Lifestyle—(living room meeting will not work where neighbors are suspicious of one another, interviews might be better).

Education/literacy—(responsive publication not advised in poorly educated neighborhood, perhaps try open house/drop-in center).

Past history—(one more survey after others have been done would be ill-advised, perhaps observation, then meetings).

Location—(interviews might be preferable to meetings with a dispersed community).

Homogeneity—(a more heterogeneous neighborhood calls for a set of methods, with several options available).

Political Considerations:

Ethics—(any method used without residents' knowledge poses ethical problems).

Empowerment—(participatory workshops will empower, surveys probably will not).

Embarrassment—(very active workshop might make reserved people feel silly, perhaps try individual interviews).

Intrusion—(activity log might be seen as more intrusive than standard survey).

Cooperation/support needed—(walking tour requires a commitment that observation does not).

Practical Considerations:

Time—(community meetings can be organized quickly, surveys can take months).

Money—(behavioral mapping's time requirement could mean high costs compared to the community meeting).

Energy—(organizing a charette takes many people's energies—a few living room meetings might be more advisable).

Skills—(anyone can do a quickie survey, but special skills are needed to stage a very participatory workshop).

Facilities/equipment—(computers might be necessary for large survey while interview data can be hand analyzed).

Project/Task Considerations:

Scope/length—(variety of methods might be called for to do full plan while few meetings would suffice to review one proposal).

Precision—(survey could yield very precise data, while meetings might produce only general preferences).

Sensitivity—(touchy issue not well dealt with at public meeting—perhaps use anonymous survey).

OVERVIEW OF STEPS IN NEIGHBORHOOD PLANNING

The actual steps involved in preparing a neighborhood plan are not very complicated in the sense that they seem to be common sense: collect information, assess it, set some goals, think up various ways to meet the goals, and select some of those. In this section, a brief overview of those tasks will be presented; the remainder of the guide will then systematically provide much more detail on each of those steps.

Step One: Collecting Information

Planners, as professionals, always like to base their plans on the best information available (though they might not always succeed in that quest). In neighborhood planning, information about the neighborhood itself and about events or forces impinging on it from the outside is collected. The categories of information range from the physical (e.g., how land is being used) to the social (e.g., the sense of community), and from the highly quantifiable (e.g., population) to the highly narrative (e.g., history of the area).

Step Two: Making Sense of the Information: Pinpointing Issues

Once all the information has been collected, the planning group needs to make some sense of it because not all of it will be in the same form nor will it all point in the same direction. Judgment is needed in pinpointing what are the main issues on which the plan should focus, be they land use conflicts, traffic problems, social service deficiencies, or whatever.

Step Three: Setting Goals

The activity of identifying issues shades easily into setting goals for the neighborhood, although that activity itself may entail a number of tasks, such as surveys or meetings, to be sure the goals are representative of the whole neighborhood.

Step Four: Coming up with Alternatives and Selecting Among Them

Any given goal set by and for the neighborhood can usually be met several different ways, through several different means. This step in planning will have your group generating various alternatives, and then selecting one or a few of them for each goal you set.

Step Five: Putting Your Plan Together

The plan you assemble will likely have some broad statements about what you want to have happen (goals), principles you want to see followed (policies), general ways to get there (strategies), specific actions to take, and maps of existing and desired conditions. Ideally, all these elements will be tightly interrelated and support one another.

Step Six: Figuring out How to Implement Your Plan

Since plans do not implement themselves, the planning group will have to figure out what it will take to get the plan implemented—e.g., what actions to take first, what resources are necessary, or where they will be found.

Step Seven: Monitoring, Evaluating, and Updating Your Plan

This phase entails keeping on top of the implementation, deciding if the plan is still feasible some time after it has been prepared, and updating it if it does not.

Please be aware that the planning process is not likely to proceed exactly as outlined, even if a professional planner is working on the job. For instance, events happen or new information becomes available which may lead your group to recycle back to an earlier step. Perhaps the city institutes a new program that leads you to rethink your goals, or a new federal program is passed, which leads you to refashion your strategies. The planning group should be flexible and ready to move backwards if need be in order to produce an even better plan, and the planner should be ready to assist the group in figuring out how to take a step back. The other fact to be aware of is that some of the seven steps do not divide very neatly; for example, issue identification and goal setting overlap, as do information collecting and making sense of that information.

WHAT IT IS GOING TO TAKE TO DO YOUR NEIGHBORHOOD PLAN

No one ever said—at least not truthfully—that doing a neighborhood plan was a piece of cake! It is going to take a good measure of time and energy, some skill, a fair amount of organization, heaps of information, and a little money. These needs will be present whether or not a professional is working with the group. Only some of those needs can be provided by the professional.

Time and Energy

The time that a neighborhood plan can consume can range from six months to a few years, depending largely on the amount of determination the planning group has and the presence or absence of professional assistance. During some phases of the process, the leaders will be meeting perhaps weekly; during other phases, there may be lulls in the activity level. Regardless of the pace, however, there needs to be a commitment on the part of the leadership to see it through. The professional who may be working with the residents can play a major role in keeping things moving and showing the progress that is being made.

Skills

The whole philosophy underlying this guide is that residents themselves can draft a neighborhood plan if they need to—but that it would be great to have professional assistance. To do that work, certain skills will need to be found somewhere—either among the residents themselves or from the professional, or from other sources, such as educational institutions or businesses. Some people will be needed who are organizers and leaders, who doggedly drive the process forward when others start to fall by the wayside. Then you will need someone who can write decently, someone who can do some graphics, and someone who is comfortable working with numbers. It is in these latter areas where help from institutions, such as colleges, can perhaps be found. But most neighborhoods have some residents who can do some of these things; it is just a matter of locating and recruiting them. Keep in mind that even if a professional is working on the job, he or she needs to try to involve residents in doing some of these tasks, if the plan is ever to be seen as theirs.

Organization

This may be the most critical element: without organization, all the skills, information, and other resources may be squandered away. At a minimum, a dedicated group of leaders is necessary; this would be a steering committee or some such entity, which keeps on top of events and orchestrates the efforts of neighbors. This group must be as representative of the composition of the neighborhood as possible in order to be legitimate. It must also make sure the initial planning group does not dwindle down to a smaller, less representative group. It is important that the leadership is not all on the shoulders of one stalwart dedicated soul: he or she will invariably burn out if that is the case. Spreading the burden around means less weight and work for each person. Again, this ingredient of organization is needed whether the residents are going it on their own or have a planner available. The planner will likely push for the creation of some kind of steering committee to give leadership to the project.

Information

Planning is, of course, very heavily based on information, and much of the planning process is devoted to its collection. There is a three-fold classification to the information needed. First, some of it is already available, maybe even nicely packaged; you just need to figure out where it is and how to gain access. Good professional planners will know the sources. Second, some information will have to be created from scratch because no one has been collecting it. The planner's professional skills come to the foreground in helping show how information can be created. Third, some information simply cannot be found or created, and you will just have to do without it. You can cut down time spent chasing down less important information if you first touch base with the city planning office to see which information they regard as most and least essential for a neighborhood plan. So, even if residents are doing the plan themselves, they should be in contact with the city's planning office on this important matter of needed information.

Money

This need is more difficult to identify with any great specificity. The cost of doing a neighborhood plan will depend on the free/donated/in-kind services you are able to garner (e.g., a local print shop that donates the printing, a group of students who analyze a survey, a supermarket that provides the refreshments for a full-day workshop). Costs will also depend on what information you can readily obtain and what information you have to collect, say, by doing a door-to-door survey. What technical assistance you can access in areas where the residents may not have the needed skills will also determine costs. At the very least, a neighborhood wanting to do its own plan will need to budget several hundred dollars. If a professional planner is working with the residents, the city should absorb all the costs, but this is something that could vary from city to city.

3

The Substance of the Plan

COLLECTING INFORMATION

SWOT Analysis

In doing a neighborhood plan, you obviously need to know about conditions within the neighborhood—what are the strengths (e.g., beautiful old trees, active citizens, or good schools) and the weaknesses (e.g., deteriorating housing, inadequate park space, or growing incidence of poverty). However, the neighborhood does not exist in isolation from the rest of the city, and events and forces from outside impinge on it. Some of those represent opportunities (e.g., a new program to help renovate houses, a proposed retail center, or city budget increases for park acquisition), while others represent threats (e.g., a new highway, a proposed polluting plant, or reduction in city services). This investigation of what is happening inside and outside the neighborhood is known as an *environmental scan*, and includes the SWOT—strengths, weaknesses, opportunities, and threats.

Items of Information Needed and Possible Sources

The neighborhood planning process looks at the neighborhood as a physical, social, and economic entity and requires various information in each of those three broad categories, with the understanding that the categories contain some overlap. The following list of 13 areas of needed information starts with the most physical ones, then the social ones, and concludes with the economic ones. The italic section following identifies some possible sources of that information. In any of these areas, the professional planner may know of additional sources of information and might be aware that some of the expected sources do not really have good, solid information. Of course, it also happens that everyone at the start thinks the information will be available, and then it turns out not to be. The only rule of thumb is: get the best information available, try to create it if it is not already available, but do not exhaust everyone in trying to track down what is never going to be found.

Natural Environmental Features. The neighborhood is located on top of a certain hunk of the natural environment, and the natural features of that setting give the neighborhood some of its character (a strength), while perhaps also representing problems (weaknesses). Can you imagine doing a plan for a San Francisco neighborhood without taking into account its marvelous set of hills or its unsteady geology? Data need to be collected about the *land form*—hills, streams, drainage areas, and the general topography. Any *geologic hazards*, such as faults or areas of erosion should be noted. The outlines of the *flood plain* are essential pieces of data as certain facilities cannot legally be constructed in flood plains. The location of existing *street trees* and other *vegetation* should be noted. The presence and patterns of *wildlife* should be included. Foothills neighborhoods or those at the edge of the city, for instance, often have visitations from deer, prairie dogs, and other wildlife. Finally, what we have done to the environment in the way of *pollution* should be detailed: air, water, soil, noise, or olfactory pollution. (See Figure 3–1 and Figure 3–2 for some examples of maps with these kinds of data.)

The United States Geologic Survey, the state department of natural resources, and the Agricultural Extension Service might all be able to provide some of the data mentioned earlier.

Existing Land Uses. On top of that natural environment, people have developed a physical neighborhood, consisting of many different types of land uses. The existing pattern of land use is one of the most crucial items of information in planning. (See Figure 3–3 and Figure 3–4 for two examples of existing land use maps.) What the planning group needs to know about the existing land uses are the *locations* and *proportions* of each of several types of use. It is also helpful to know what *recent changes* have occurred in that patterning, such as homes being converted to offices, or retail use spreading in a certain direction. Any *planned changes* that are known about at this time should be noted, for example, some institution's plan to acquire land for a parking lot, or a senior housing development that is about to break ground. Whatever data can be obtained about *patterns of ownership* would also be useful. Are there large parcels owned by an out-of-town speculator? Is someone slowly assembling ownership of a full block? Which parcels are publicly owned?

Some of the usual categories of land use follow. Next to each one in parentheses is the color agreed on by planners to indicate the type of land use on your map.

Residential
　Single-family detached (lemon yellow)
　Duplex (pale yellow)
　Multifamily (dark brown)
　Special residential facilities, e.g. group homes (light brown)
　Mobile homes (light purple)
　Motels/hotels (purple)
Commercial—perhaps neighborhood-serving (pink) distinguished from regional-serving (dark orange)
　Retail, e.g., grocer, boutique, pharmacy (pink or dark orange)
　Services, e.g., cleaner, barber, and shoe repair (pink or dark orange)
　Offices (reddish orange)
Industrial
　Light (light grey)
　Heavy (black)
　Railroads (dark grey)
　Utilities, e.g., power stations, and water tanks (light grey)
Public
　Parks (true green)
　Schools (sky blue)
　Other public buildings, e.g., library or community center (dark green)
Semi-public
　Churches (dark blue)
　Schools—nonproprietary ones (dark blue)
　Other (lighter blue)
Vacant lands (no color)

The city's planning office may already have, and thus can provide, base maps in various levels of detail (e.g., different scales, showing outlines of structures), which may only need updating through field observation. The building department should have information about recently filed building permits and recently pulled demoli-

Figure 3–1. Natural Features Map A

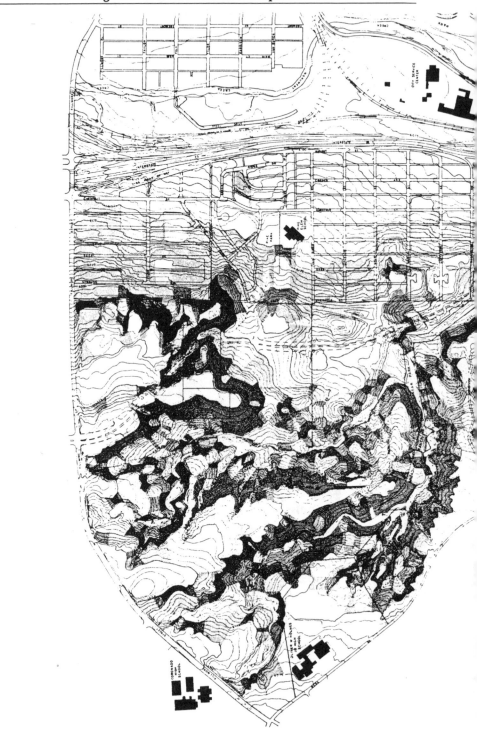

SLOPE
ANALYSIS

MESA SPRINGS
COMMUNITY PLAN

Colorado Spring Planning Department-
Mesa Springs Community Association

0 to 8%
8 to 16%
16 to 24%
Over 24%

Figure 3–2. Natural Features Map B

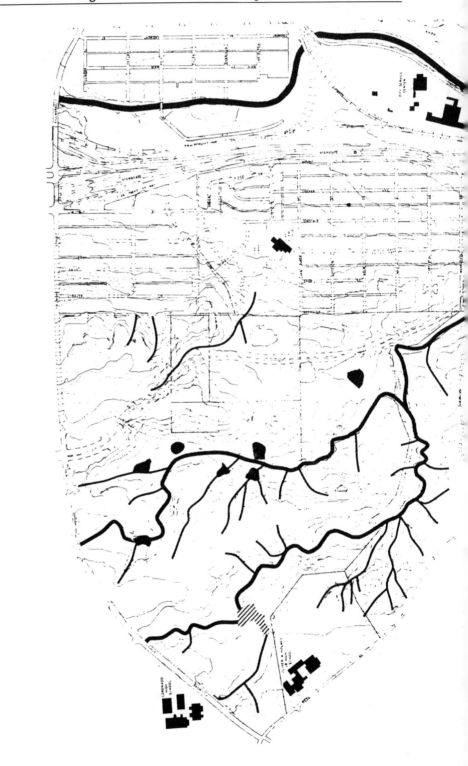

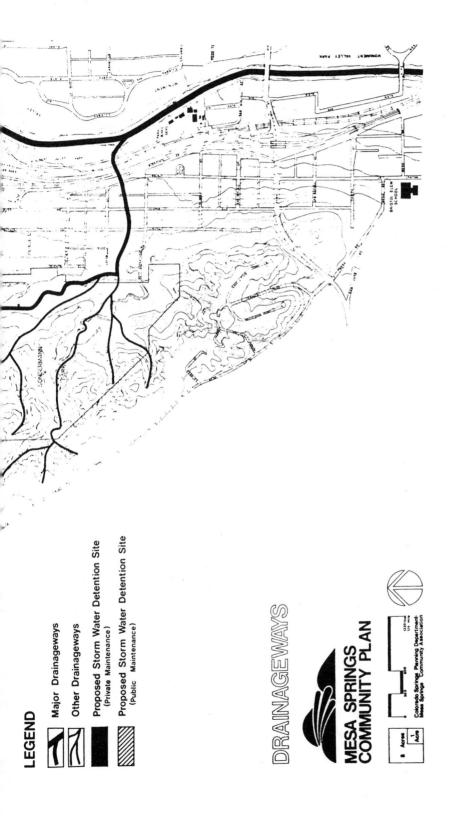

LEGEND

Major Drainageways

Other Drainageways

Proposed Storm Water Detention Site
(Private Maintenance)

Proposed Storm Water Detention Site
(Public Maintenance)

DRAINAGEWAYS

MESA SPRINGS
COMMUNITY PLAN

Colorado Springs Planning Department-
Mesa Springs Community Association

Figure 3-3. Existing Land Uses Map A

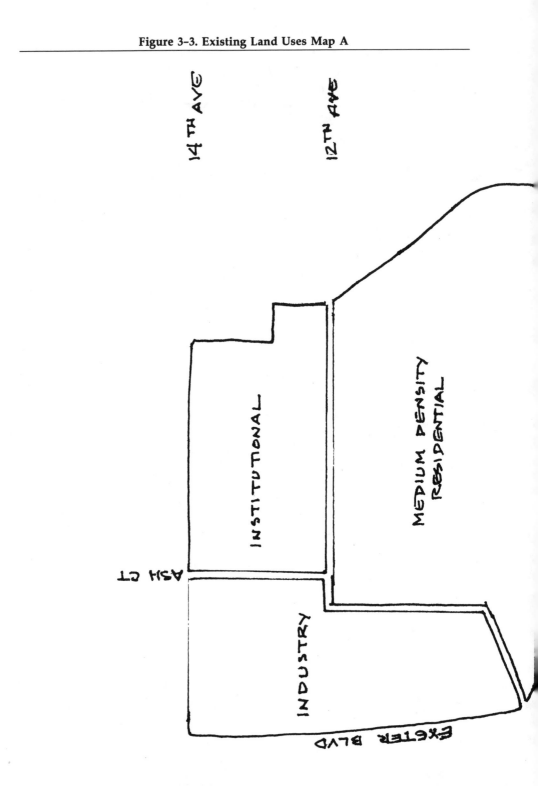

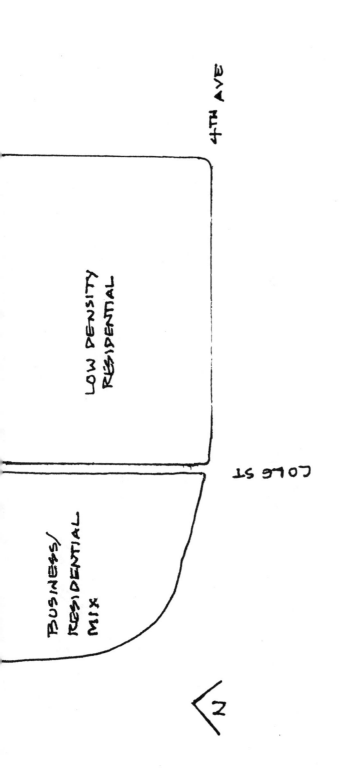

Dominant Land Uses

On this land use map, only the *general* areas where given types of land use predominate have been indicated. This gives an *overview* picture of the neighborhood's land use, whereas the next map illustrates a more detailed picture of the land use in a given area.

Figure 3–4. Existing Land Uses Map B

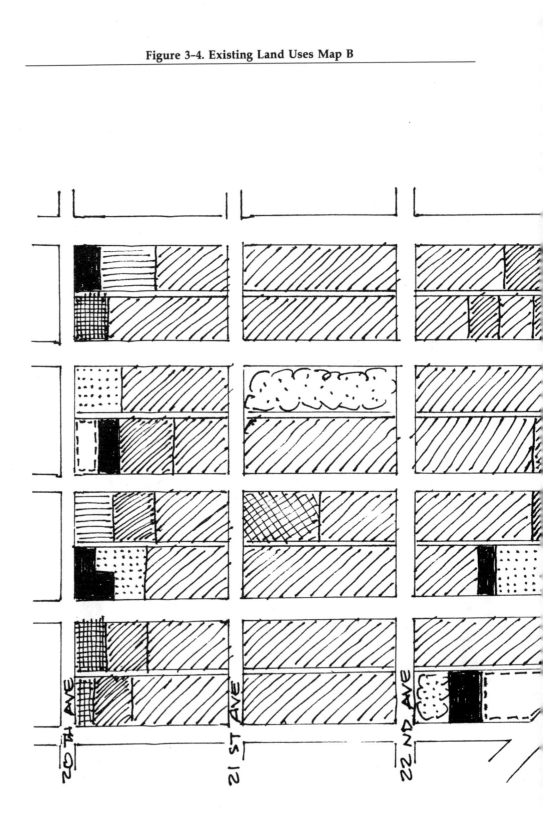

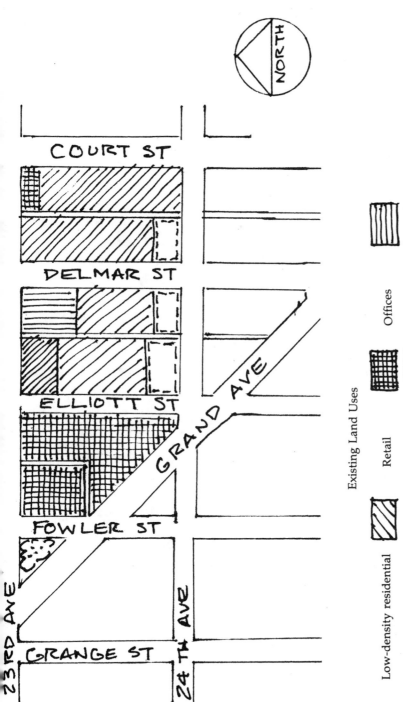

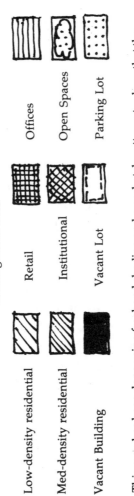

Existing Land Uses

Low-density residential	Offices
Med-density residential	Open Spaces
Vacant Building	Parking Lot
Retail	
Institutional	
Vacant Lot	

This map has been done using freehand shading and crosshatch patterns to show that the store-bought zipatone used on most other maps, while nice, is not necessary.

tion permits. The assessor's office will have data about ownership, but you'll proba-bly first have to narrow down the area and be ready to devote many hours to the task.

Zoning. In most cities of any size, each and every parcel of land has been designated by the local government with a certain zoning category, which identifies what uses are permitted (and, in effect, what uses are not permitted) on that piece of land. At this point of the process, you do not need to be concerned with all the possible uses; all you need to worry about is what is the *existing zoning*, such as R-2 (two-family dwelling), OC (office complex), C-6 (general business), or whatever set of designations are used in your city. You should also, however, make note of *recent changes* that have been made in zoning, as well as any major *variances* (where an otherwise nonpermitted use is allowed to occur under some special circumstances or with special restrictions). In addition—and this starts to move the planning team into analysis—data should be collected about the *compatibility or incompatibility between the zoning and the actual land use.* Is there any office in an area zoned for residential use? Does the zoning call for high density residences that were once expected to de-velop, but which have not? Figure 3–5 shows an example of a map of ex-isting zoning.

The zoning administration should be able to provide most of these items of information.

Circulation. This area of data gathering looks at movement—how people get around, into, and out of the neighborhood, whether driving, walking, taking the bus, or whatever. Public officials responsible for the streets in a city (transportation planners and traffic engineers) usually classify streets into a three-part hierarchy. *Arterial streets* carry large amounts of vehicles (perhaps 10,000 or more vehicles per day) which are usually allowed to move rapidly and without much interruption (i.e., few stop lights or stop signs). They are mainly for crosstown traffic or move-ment between major activity centers. *Collectors* are streets with a lesser traffic volume (say 2,000–10,000 vehicles per day and more traffic con-trols) that link arterials to local streets. Those *local streets* carry even less traffic (under 2,000 vehicles per day) and will have slower posted speeds and more traffic control devices. They are more likely to be discontinu-ous, that is, may not go very far before they bump into something like a park or a collector street. How many vehicles per day are used as the cut-off points in defining streets will vary from city to city: a street that residents in a city of 120,000 think is busy (an arterial) may be a local street by Los Angeles standards! Some cities will also add subcategories, such as major or minor arterials and major or minor collectors.

Other data about streets that should be noted include the location of state and federal highways (because the city is less free to alter anything there), truck routes, and one-way streets. Still other useful information, if it can be gathered, would be average speed levels and accident rates, at least on the arterial streets. Finally, the extent of curb cuts for the disabled should be noted.

So, in addition to categorizing each street in the neighborhood, the planning group should also indicate known changes and plans, and if possible, indicate the *volume-to-capacity ratio*. That piece of data may or may not be available from the city. What it indicates is whether a street is carrying a traffic load in excess of what it was designed to carry, or whether it has room for more (referred to as *excess capacity*—music to a traffic engineer's ears).

The information about circulation should also include information about *mass transit*—where the routes are, where the stops are located, known changes and plans. Finally, *pedestrian and bike routes*—both formally designated ones and informal ones—should be identified. An illustrative map showing circulation data is shown in Figure 3–6.

> *The planning or public works departments will have most of these items of information. Also the state highway department would have data on any of their system that runs through your neighborhood. The public transit agency can provide data on their system. Observation will be required for information on pedestrian and bike routes (unless the city has designated bike routes).*

Utilities. The utilities in a neighborhood include a number of systems that are crucial, although often out of sight and out of mind. They include storm and sanitary sewers, water lines, gas lines, power lines, telephone wiring, and cable wiring. In each case, what is needed is a map of the network, as well as statements of any known changes or plans.

> *Public works department, utility companies, and the cable company should possess these data.*

Housing. From the point of view of residents, clearly one of the most important elements of a neighborhood is its housing stock. There are many things anyone doing a neighborhood plan needs to ascertain about

Figure 3–5. Map of Existing Zoning

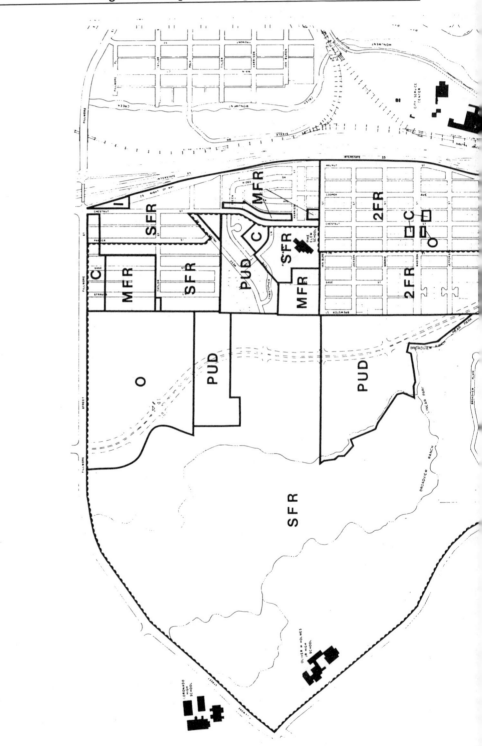

PUD — Planned Unit Development

SFR — Single Family Residential
(R, R-1-6000, R-1-9000)

2FR — Two Family Residential
(R-2)

MFR — Multi Family Residential
(R-4, R-5)

O — Office (OR, OC)

C — Commercial (C-5, C-6, PBC)

I — Industrial (M-1, M-2, PIP)

— Hillside Area Overlay

EXISTING
ZONING

MESA SPRINGS
COMMUNITY PLAN

Colorado Springs Planning Department
Mesa Springs Community Association

Figure 3-6. Circulation Map

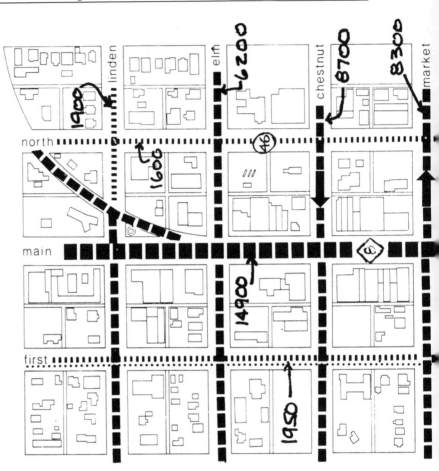

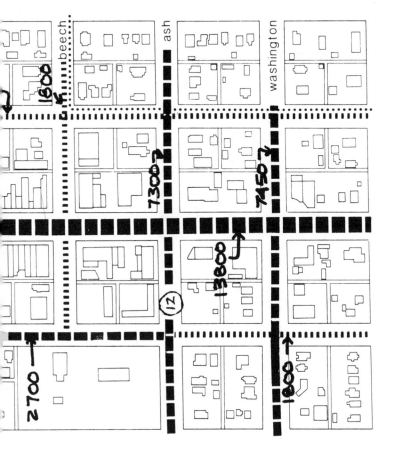

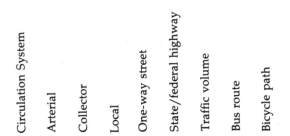

N

Circulation System

Arterial

Collector

Local

One-way street

State/federal highway

Traffic volume

Bus route

Bicycle path

the area's housing. The land use inventory will already have identified where housing is and the general types (from single family detached to mobile homes). Do not forget to collect data on any public housing in the area.

To get a fuller grasp of the situation, data about housing styles should be noted (e.g., mainly brick, one-story bungalows; three-story walk-up apartments of a certain design; and townhouses in a southwestern style). Then, too, knowing the year of construction of the neighborhood's housing stock gives the planning group some indicators of a possible need for rehabilitation. Your map might indicate general areas where the housing is of a certain vintage, if you cannot obtain data on a building-by-building basis.

That data need brings us into the area of housing conditions. Unfortunately, there are no clear-cut criteria available to use, but some simply, agreed-on categories could be devised, such as "very good," "acceptable or fair," and "in need of maintenance." If there are any programs of rehabilitation already in operation in the area, the areas where those are occurring should be noted. In addition, the status of the neighborhood in the city's official housing assistance plan should be mentioned. This is a document the city needs to have on file for the U.S. Department of Housing and Urban Development if it wishes to seek Community Development Block Grant (CDBG) funds. Any plans that either the city, developers, or others have for the area should be included in this section.

It is important to get a sense of what trends are going on with regard to the neighborhood's housing. Several kinds of data will give information on this trend. First, how much, if any, new housing construction has there been in the area over the last number of years, say ten? Second, what are sales prices for housing doing over the last few years? Third, what are rental rates like over that same period of time? Fourth, and last, what is the vacancy rate for both owned and rental units. (See Figures 3–7 and 3–8 for some examples of maps with housing data.)

Many sources of information about housing are available: the U.S. census for basic numbers, the assessor's office for date of construction and ownership, realtors for sales and price data, the building department for construction permit data, the housing authority for public housing information. The planning office may also have some useful information already assembled. Sometimes, lenders keep data about rental vacancies, or an apartment owners' association may record that.

Community Facilities and Services. A number of different kinds of physical structures and structured programs/services play a role in giving a neighborhood its amenity level; collectively, these are referred to as community facilities and services. The planning team will want to determine the presence or absence of each of these facilities, its specific location, its general level of adequacy, and any plans for future changes. (See Figure 3–9 for a sample map.)

- Schools
- Libraries and museums
- Community centers
- Social service facilities
- Hospital and medical offices
- Parks and recreation centers
- Police and fire stations
- Post office
- Churches
- Any other similar structure

Among the services or programs about which data should be collected include the following:

- Police and fire protection
- Schools, including adult/continuing education
- Health and mental health programs
- Social services (e.g., child care, youth programs, senior programs, and basic public assistance programs)
- Recreational programs
- Cultural arts programs

Some of this information will have been gathered during the land use inventory. If not, field observation can pick it up. Interviews with representatives of the various agencies would also be helpful. The United Way would have an overview of social services in the area, and police and fire departments can also provide some of what is needed.

Urban Design Features. This aspect of the neighborhood inventory requires greater analysis while the data are being collected. In addition, there is an element of judgment about it, and the judgment of a professional planner may be really helpful at this stage. Urban design features relates to the way the neighborhood's many physical elements appear as they relate to one another and add up (or fail to add up) to an overall coherent image that stays in your mind. Still sounds foggy, right? Let's illustrate with examples of physical elements that might be observed under

Figure 3–7. Housing Map A

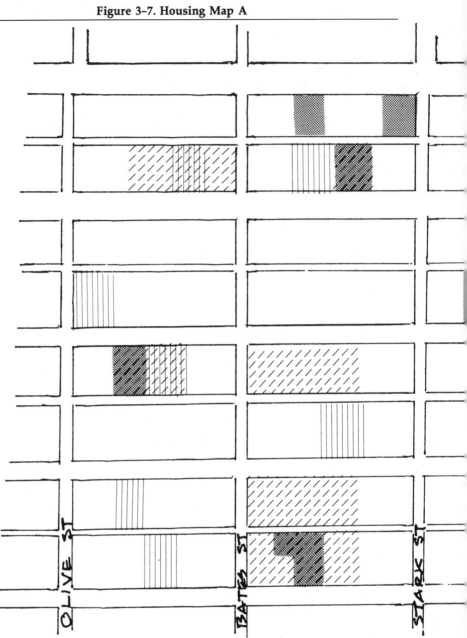

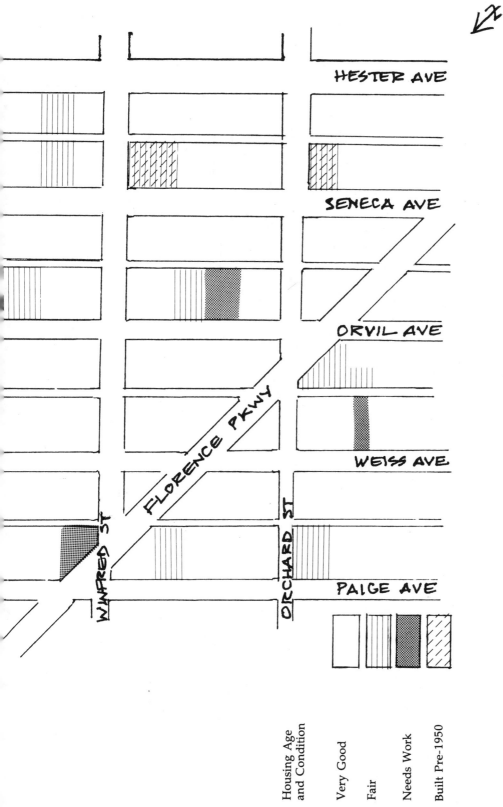

HESTER AVE

SENECA AVE

ORVIL AVE

FLORENCE PKWY

WEISS AVE

WINFRED ST

ORCHARD ST

PAIGE AVE

Housing Age
and Condition

Very Good

Fair

Needs Work

Built Pre-1950

Figure 3–8. Housing Map B

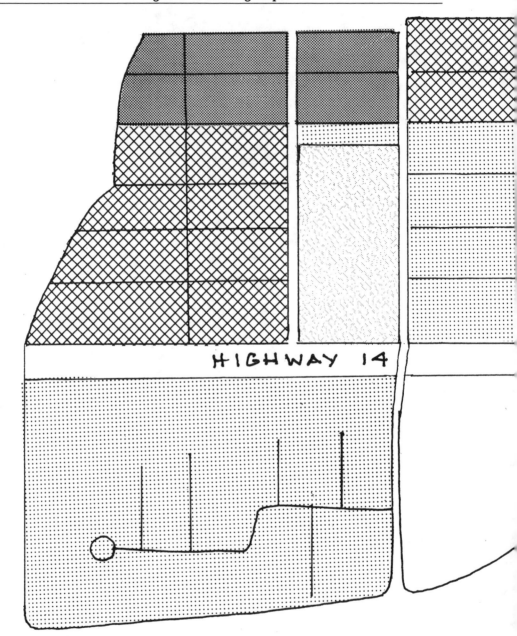

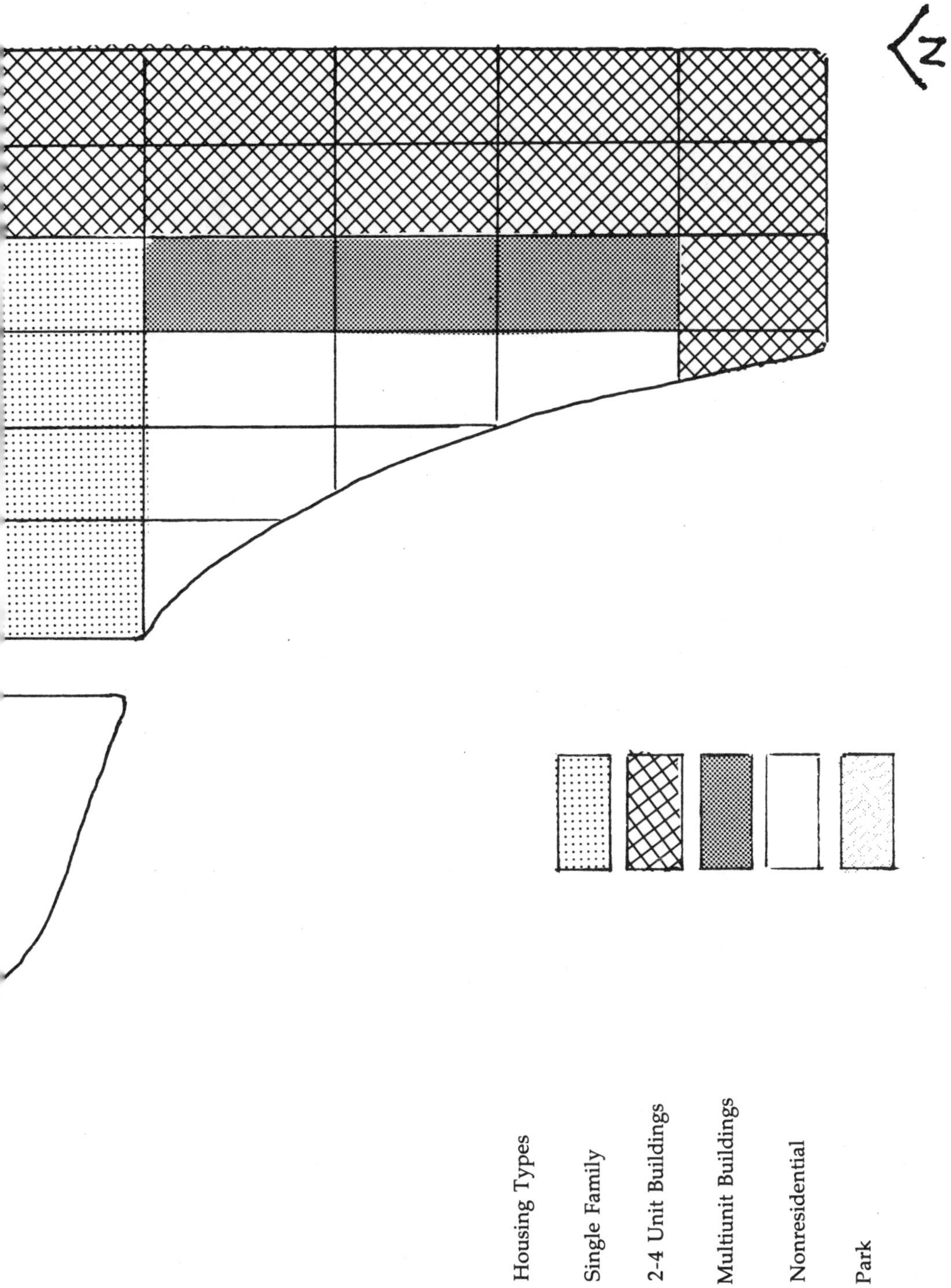

Housing Types

Single Family

2-4 Unit Buildings

Multiunit Buildings

Nonresidential

Park

Figure 3-9. Community Facilities and Services Map

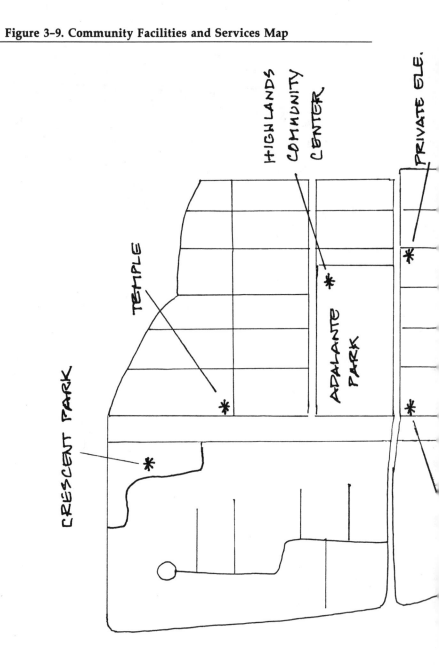

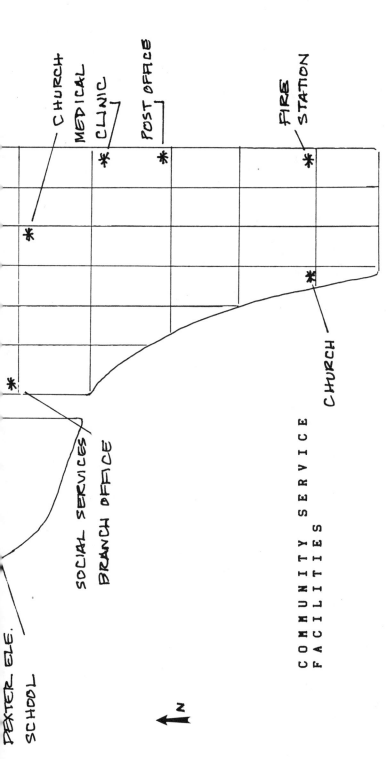

CHURCH

MEDICAL CLINIC

POST OFFICE

FIRE STATION

CHURCH

PEXTER ELE. SCHOOL

SOCIAL SERVICES BRANCH OFFICE

N

COMMUNITY SERVICE FACILITIES

this category. Any significant structures or sites would be included, such as a gracious old mansion, a series of quaint row houses, several blocks of houses designed and constructed at the same time that typify the neighborhood. Special attention should be directed to the design fabric of the neighborhood, the identification of any structures or areas already designated as historical landmarks, as well as to any that have not been designated, but may warrant it.

Part of the urban design scheme consists of any special views, such as a tree-shaded boulevard, a prominent peak which is framed by several attractive houses, or tight and narrow streets which present visual surprises each time you turn a corner. Sometimes a neighborhood has something like a *gateway*—a certain street you enter that clearly introduces you to the neighborhood and defines where it begins and ends. Those beginnings and endings—the neighborhood's *edges*—are another urban design feature. Some neighborhoods have clean and crisp edges, while others blur into the adjacent area. What is it that tells you you are now in your neighborhood? Whatever that is might be a significant urban design feature.

A big part of a neighborhood's urban design character derives from the characteristics of buildings, such as height, width, depth, and architectural style. The *scale* of buildings is important: do they dwarf and intimidate you or are they comfortable to be near? What materials were used in their construction? Is there a theme (e.g., tudor framing, southwestern adobe, or New England clapboard)? The relationship of buildings to the street also contributes to a neighborhood's design flavor—are houses uniformly set back from the street, do they come practically up to the curb, or are they varied?

The neighborhood may have within it some distinct *subareas,* where the street pattern (e.g., grid versus curved or wide versus narrow) changes or where the type of houses dramatically changes. Such distinctions help define the image of the neighborhood. Perhaps there are prominent activity centers, such as a shopette where you always run into people you know, or a post office next to a grocery store that is an informal gathering place. These too give a neighborhood its urban design character.

The reader running these images through the mind and turning up nothing need not be overly worried. Part of the planning process is to create an urban design character if one is lacking, or enhance what is there. In addition, ferreting out that character may come only through conversation, where one person's observations trigger a spark in another, who then starts to see the neighborhood in a new light. The important thing is to have identified the opportunities that exist for creating or enhancing that image. (A map with urban design data can be seen in Figure 3–10.)

Direct observation will probably yield the best data here, especially if done through something like a group walk through the neighborhood, followed by a discussion. Another technique is to have everyone take a roll of photos of aspects of the neighborhood they consider memorable, have them developed, and then share them all as part of the group discussion. While experts in the design and planning field may have some sophisticated notions about what constitutes good urban design, ultimately it is the residents who will have to live with whatever aesthetic character is included in the plan. The professional, however, can help residents identify and give names to what is special, such as by bringing in pictures exemplifying the urban design character of other neighborhoods, or arranging a bus tour of another neighborhood.

General Physical Conditions. A planning group might want to collect a number of items of information about physical environmental conditions that strongly contribute to neighborhood satisfaction or (more likely) dissatisfaction: trash, unpaved alleys, broken sidewalks, trees in need of trimming or replacement, potholes, and vacant, unkempt lots.

Basically, direct observation will give the best results here, although some city agencies (e.g., public works, health, and sanitation) may be helpful.

History. As we move from purely physical issues to more social ones, the history of the neighborhood is the first item to investigate. The point of recounting the area's history is to strengthen the neighborhood's identity by providing an understanding of where the neighborhood came from, what has been its uniqueness, what role has it played within the whole city's story, what from the past can be built on for the future. Learning for the first time that some famous person was born there may provide a theme or image if the neighborhood seems to lack one now. Finding that the neighborhood was laid out on top of an old cemetery presents intriguing possibilities. Sometimes this search turns up a name for the neighborhood that no one had ever heard of before, and which sounds better than the one currently in use.

The public library will probably be the single most helpful source, but others would be state, county, and local historical societies, a university history department, and the local newspaper's morgue (its old files). Do not forget to consult the informal neighborhood historian who's lived there many years . . . and maybe has never been asked to tell the neighborhood's story! Telling stories about the neighborhood can be

Figure 3–10. Urban Design Features Map

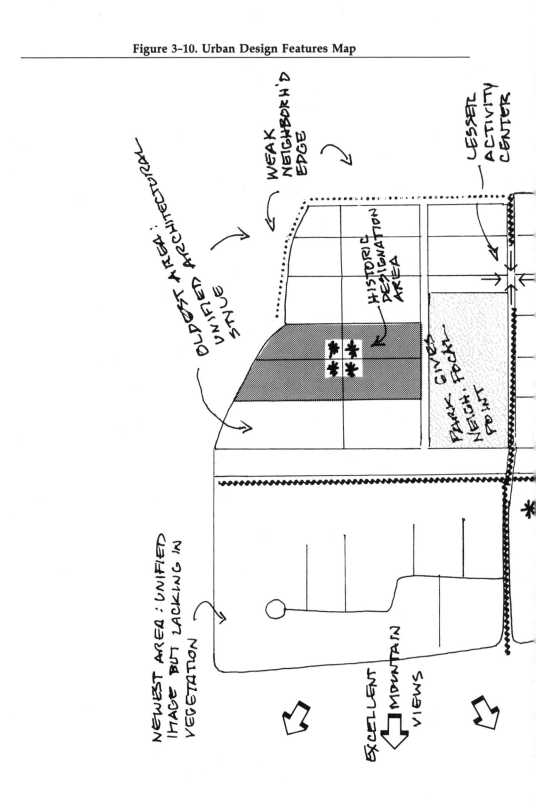

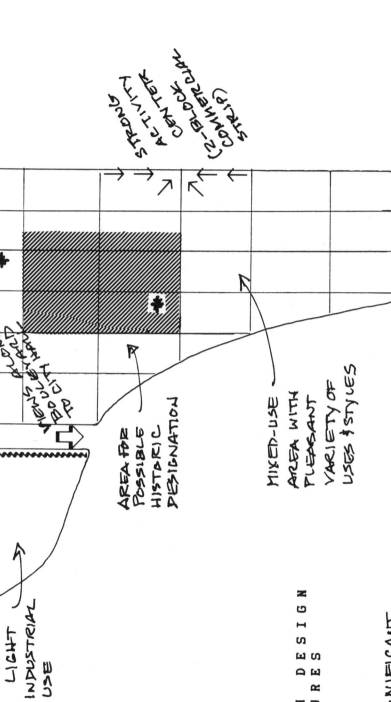

STRONG ACTIVITY CENTER (2-BLOCK COMMERCIAL STRIP)

VIEWS ALONG BOULEVARD TO CITY

AREA FOR POSSIBLE HISTORIC DESIGNATION

MIXED-USE AREA WITH PLEASANT VARIETY OF USES & STYLES

LIGHT INDUSTRIAL USE

N

URBAN DESIGN FEATURES

✳ SIGNIFICANT STRUCTURES

*a wonderful tool for turning up little-known information, while giving many peo-
ple, who may have thought they had nothing to contribute, a real opportunity to
make a contribution.*

Demography. This is a fancy term for population characteristics. This
is where the planning group gets to talk about the people who reside in
the neighborhood. A number of different population characteristics
should be investigated, and in each case, it is helpful to compare your
neighborhood to the rest of the city, and to show the parallel data for
1960, 1970, and 1980, and any projections of later data. (Census data for
1990 will be available probably in 1992.) Those analyses give some picture of what may be special about your neighborhood and how it has
been evolving. Depending on the boundaries of the neighborhood, there
may be parts of several census tracts within the neighborhood, which
allow some distinctions among parts of the neighborhood to be drawn. In
any case, the effort should be made to get data for the smallest subareas
possible. (See Tables 3–1, 3–2, and 3–3 for some examples of demographic data.)

Table 3–1. Total Population

| | Melville Neighborhood | | City | |
Year	Number	% Change	Number	% Change
1960	2,719	—	127,601	—
1970	2,912	7.1	184,537	44.6
1980	3,001	3.1	212,437	15.1
1990(proj.)	3,700	23.3	248,198	16.8

Table 3–1 shows that while the city's overall population growth moder-
ated after 1970, the Melville neighborhood, which had been trailing behind the overall city growth rate, is expected to show a substantial gain
during the 1980s.

Table 3–2. Age Composition

	Melville Neighborhood	City
Under 18	20.4%	26.9%
19 - 29	22.1	24.4
30 - 39	18.1	15.4
40 - 49	16.3	14.8
50 - 59	13.4	10.9
60 +	9.7	7.6

Table 3–2 shows that the Melville neighborhood is generally older than the city as a whole.

Table 3–3. Occupied Housing Units and Density

	Melville Neighborhood	City
Total Pop.	3001	212,437
Total Housing Units	1219	81,393
Persons per Unit	2.46	2.61

Table 3–3 shows that, on the average, the Melville neighborhood has fewer persons per occupied housing unit than the city.

The most important population characteristics to be described are:

- Total population
- Age: distribution, mean, median, percent under 18 and over 65
- Sex: distribution
- Ethnicity: distribution
- Special populations, such as the physically disabled, single heads of household, institutionalized persons
- Housing: total units, number of households
- Persons per household
- Density: persons per acre
- Mobility/stability: distribution of lengths of residence, percent in the same house five years ago
- Education: distribution, average number of years, drop-out rate
- Occupation: distribution, percent unemployed
- Income: distribution, median, percent below poverty level

The U.S. Census is without doubt the best source here. In addition, the planning department may have prepared some useful reports based on census data and may do projections between census periods, although probably not down to the level of neighborhoods.

Social Analysis. Unless a community survey has been done, data for this section may be rather sparse. Nevertheless, it is a crucial area to cover, because it moves beyond the demographic data and starts to say what kind of place this is in which to live. Items that might be included here start with an assessment of the *quality of life*, which can be derived from data already discussed—e.g., amenities available, quality of the housing neighborhood aesthetics, income, and unemployment.

A second area to look into is *sense of community*: do people know one another, do they even talk to one another, do they help one another, is there a viable and effective neighborhood organization, are there manifestations of pride in the neighborhood, are there shared symbols?

Arlene Hetherington, who consults with rural communities on tourism issues, helps them find what she calls the *heart and soul* of the community, a third item to identify. This heart and soul is a physical as well as an intangible thing: it may be a particular place of importance, like those identified in the urban design section, or it may be an informal group of retired people who hang out at the park, or a certain symbol that everyone recognizes and uses.

Fourth, you might try to describe the *political climate* in the sense of organizations where collective decisionmaking goes on (e.g., neighborhood organization, strong precinct groups, or lodges), the forms of political life (e.g., a lot of organized activity versus everybody acting on their own), and the climate (conservative to progressive, active to passive, very unified to very fractured, or high versus low voter turnout).

Direct observation and group discussion, supplemented by some interviews, would prove most useful here.

Economic Base. For most neighborhoods, the most visible forms of economic activity consist of small stores and offices; clearly, some neighborhoods have more, such as factories, major shopping centers or strips, and office parks. Whatever form it takes, economic activity plays a big role in shaping the neighborhood. Thus, data should be collected about the major economic activities and their location. Special attention should be given to the presence in the neighborhood of major employers, whether in the private, public, or nonprofit sector. In addition, data should be gathered about the labor force (kinds of occupations, pay levels, and unemployment), and about the residents' purchasing power. This latter item is of great interest to any retailer you might be trying to attract to the neighborhood.

The biggest challenge here is in finding data that's neighborhood-specific: in some cases, you will be lucky to find data at the city level. But you might obtain useful information from the state's department of labor and employment, university researchers, the county's tax collector, the better business bureau, the chamber of commerce, as well as through direct observation.

Priorities in Information Collecting

While all the items of information listed earlier contribute to a more comprehensive understanding of the neighborhood, there are certain ones that the city's planning office would probably regard as most essential. Those are existing land use, zoning, circulation, housing, community facilities, and demography. Those happen to be the ones that are generally most readily available and nicely quantifiable. The neighborhood planning team, however, is urged to collect as much information in the other categories as possible because the neighborhood is not just a physical place, as the list of priority items might suggest. A useful strategy might be to outline all the information needs, determine which are readily available, which are ones you will have to develop on your own (through field surveys, interviews, and so on), and which seem impossible to obtain. Then set your priorities based on that map of the data. It is acknowledged that the smaller the city, the fewer will be the number of public and private agencies collecting data, and, therefore, the harder it will be to find what information you want.

A crucial role the professional planner plays in working on a neighborhood plan is in knowing somewhat more about what data are available and how to gain access to them. The planner should function here as a conduit to other public entities which might be more responsive to a request from fellow city staffer than from the citizens. Perhaps the planner takes along a resident, who then gets to meet the other staff personally; that can lead to opening the channels for citizens as indeed they should be.

MAKING SENSE OF THE INFORMATION: PINPOINTING ISSUES

Analysis and Assessment of Information

The plan your planning group eventually drafts will be only as good as the information on which it is based and the analysis of that information. Once all the information has been collected (remembering that there may not be a smooth end point to that prior phase), the planning group sits down and starts to sort through it. Clearly one way to organize the information is by the categories named in the previous section, or by the SWOT categories. But there may be other ways to slice the pie as well. If some data are available on a block-by-block basis, you may be able to pinpoint certain blocks where the data suggest problems. Creating new categories, that cut across the formal ones, may prove useful, such as "things we like," "things we dislike," "attractive things," "ugly things," "too many," or "too few." Once you have created such categories, then look at the data, and write down key points within each category. The temptation at this point, perhaps especially among the residents, is to drift into goal-setting. It is suggested you resist this temptation and focus on analyzing and assessing, because that will lead the way into goal-setting very quickly and with greater clarity.

A very useful way to see what the data contains is to plot some of them on maps, simply writing little notes at the appropriate locations on the map, such as "very congested intersection," or "too many tacky storefronts," or "great views of river from here." Rather than use up many maps, you can purchase plastic (acetate) sheets, which can be taped over the map. One overlay might focus on land use, another on traffic, a third on aesthetics, and so on.

Another way to organize the information for presentation and future utility is by preparing briefing papers that pull together (in the space of one or two pages) the key points about a given issue (e.g., transportation) and identify some of the choices that need to be made. The briefing paper does not usually suggest which choice should be made, but says, "Here's the issue, here is the existing situation, and here are some areas in which we have got to make some decisions."

Categorizing Your Neighborhood

Planners often devise sets of categories for neighborhoods that assist them as they look across the city at different neighborhoods, trying to figure out general strategies that can help several similar neighborhoods at once. This same practice can assist your planning team understand what kind of neighborhood yours is. One classification uses these terms: developing (new neighborhoods), redeveloping (undergoing some big changes), stable (holding its own, not experiencing any dramatic change), and declining (experiencing real problems). Another set of categories, more descriptive than judgmental, consists of:

- **Community:** large, well-known district, recognized by outsiders as one area, but which has internal subareas of some importance to residents.
- **Old established neighborhood:** an older area, often having a distinct ethnic flavor and rich traditions.

- **Outlying neighborhood:** a less urbanized, recently annexed area of the city.
- **Mixed land use neighborhood:** a neighborhood that has within its boundaries large sections of land devoted to industrial, commercial, institutional, or highway use.
- **Strictly residential neighborhood:** an area, often bound by arterial streets with commercial use, but having within the area no land uses but residential ones, except for a school, church, or small grocery store.
- **Residential enclave:** a minute cluster of homes, which is isolated physically and probably socially from the rest of the community; often adjacent to, if not surrounded by, industrial or highway uses.

In attempting to categorize your neighborhood, you will probably find yourselves looking most closely at such data as land use, changes in zoning, residential turnover, and income. Still, the process is rather judgmental. Just make sure there has been ample discussion so that the judgment represents a consensus. Again, the professional planner can prove useful as an information source, supplying categories the city may already use, or reports from other cities that may help in this activity.

Ways to Integrate Information

One step beyond analysis and assessment is the integration of data, where several different kinds of information are pushed together to see if they tell you something more in combination than any one did on its own. One useful technique here is *scenario-building*, which is the act of composing a picture of what the neighborhood might be like at some point in the future (e.g., five, ten years) if certain trends are continued, or are reversed. For example, a planning group might project that given the heavy arterial traffic, and the steady decline in homeownership that they are currently seeing along certain blocks, in five years the neighborhood would experience pressure for rezoning from residential to commercial as some streets become increasingly undesirable places to live. Then, that picture, that scenario, could be fleshed out some more: such as, what would be the impact on schools or on retail stores. Another group might look at what might be expected to happen if new development keeps occurring at the edge of the neighborhood. In each case, several scenarios might be prepared, based on different assumptions, such as no growth in traffic in that first example, versus 5 percent growth, versus 10 percent growth, and so on. The experiences of other cities, which have seen similar trends, would prove useful, if such information can be supplied by the planner.

Another technique that could help pull together information is the *profile*, which is a composite of several key items of data. This might be done for a neighborhood that has two or three subareas (see Table 3–4).

Table 3–4. Profiles

Feature	Subarea 1	Subarea 2	Subarea 3
Population	Mostly young families in first homes	Mixed, very transient	Older families now being replaced by younger ones
Housing	Strong, new for most part	Showing signs of deterioration	Aging, but generally stable
Open space	New developments include open spaces	The few spaces are not well maintained	One strong area, but otherwise deficient
Aesthetics	Monotonous character	Chaotic, no unified image	Generally gracious

Yet another way to pull data together is by using *maps*, like those mentioned earlier, but now combined into one map that shows the key issues. Using magic markers, draw in some circles, a few arrows, and any other symbols that seem useful and communicate clearly your sense of what the neighborhood is like. If you prepared some acetate overlays, tape several of them on top of your base map at one time. That should give you some new perspectives (as long as you can still see the base map underneath!).

Displaying Information

Your planning team can display information in narrative paragraphs, tables of numbers, maps, and other visual displays. Information most suited to narrative presentation would be the history of the neighborhood, the social analysis, and descriptions of community services available. Some of the information that would go well in table form are the demographics, economic base data, and circulation data. Maps work well for displaying data about land use, zoning, community facilities, and housing conditions. Do not let these suggestions, however, constrain your creativity in arriving at new and different ways to display what you have discovered. One neighborhood planner I know asks residents to prepare drawings, songs, and poems that tell the story of the neighborhood.

In each case of displaying information, the map, chart, table, or whatever should be done with the greatest amount of expertise available. If there is a professional planner working on the project, that person should probably do them, sharing expertise along the way. If no planner is involved, residents will need to do the work on their own to the best of their abilities. Do not overlook expertise you might find in your own backyard, however, in the form of volunteers.

Narratives. Narratives should use short, punchy sentences and, following the dictates of our grade school teachers, "tell 'em what you gonna tell 'em, tell 'em, and then tell 'em what you told 'em." If you're not a planner, do not try to write like one, but do use a vocabulary that has some precision to it. Most of the terms you will ever need appear in this guide and have been explained. If you are a planner, forget the jargon you learned in school, and go back to basic English!

Tables. In constructing tables, keep them simple: better to have several tables, each with one or two items of information than complex ones which try to report umpteen things at once. Tables generally have a standard format: the things you want to report information about are on the left side of the table, and the features that you want to report about those things are strung out across the top. The example above reverses that because there will be too many features (such as, housing, open space) to fit on any page going across. A sample format is shown in Table 3–5.

Table 3–5. Sample Table

Zoning Categories	Number of Parcels	Percent of Total
R-1	412	42.9%
R-2	116	12.1
C-6	89	9.3
etc.		

Maps. The size of the map scale depends on the size of the neighborhood and the size of the paper you wish to use in your final document, but generally you will want to use the largest scale map you can when recording raw information (e.g., 1″ = 200′). Whatever you use is likely to be reduced down when you print it. For much of the data you might want to show, a *street map* will suffice: that shows the outline of each block. Sometimes you need a more detailed map, such as a *parcel map* that shows the size and shape of each parcel of land and the outline (footprint) of the structure that sits upon it.

How one actually displays information on a map depends on the data to be shown and how fancy you wish to get. Colored markers do a wonderful job for many kinds of data: three colors for three levels of housing conditions, varied colors for land use categories (standardized, as noted earlier), different thicknesses of streets depending on traffic volume, and so on. Often just circling some site and writing in some words can tell the story; or perhaps arrows to show the direction of bicycle traffic or special views. Arrows are also often used to show pressure, such as business encroachment on a residential area. Examples of maps of different types at a 1″ = 1000′ scale can be seen in Figures 3–11, 3–12 and 3–13.

Visual Displays. Other techniques include photographs (which can have arrows pointing to a feature, with a written note off to one side), freehand sketches (that allow you to discard details that confuse the issue and focus on a particular point you wish to highlight), and videotaping (a largely untapped medium in neighborhood planning). An amateur with some skills, using a video tape recorder, could, for example, construct an eye-opening tour of the neighborhood, or a survey of different housing styles.

NOTE: These figures contain maps of the same neighborhood; each map shows progressively more detail, and thus each is most appropriate for showing some particular kinds of information. All the maps are at the same scale, namely, 1″ = 1000 feet. Figure 3–11 has only the outlines of the blocks. This would be suitable for the most general information, such as natural environmental features, circulation, utility networks, and community facilities and services.

Figure 3–12 has each parcel of land outlined. This kind of map is suitable for mapping land use, zoning, and general physical conditions; it allows pinpointing of data to particular pieces of land, as illustrated by the shading in of some parcels on the map.

Figure 3–13 adds yet another level of detail, namely, the outline (footprint) of each structure. Housing and urban design data might well require this level of detail for mapping, such as showing the different densities of structures in the subareas or showing where housing rehabilitation work is needed.

Figure 3–11. Neighborhood Map A

Figure 3–12. Neighborhood Map B

Figure 3–13. Neighborhood Map C

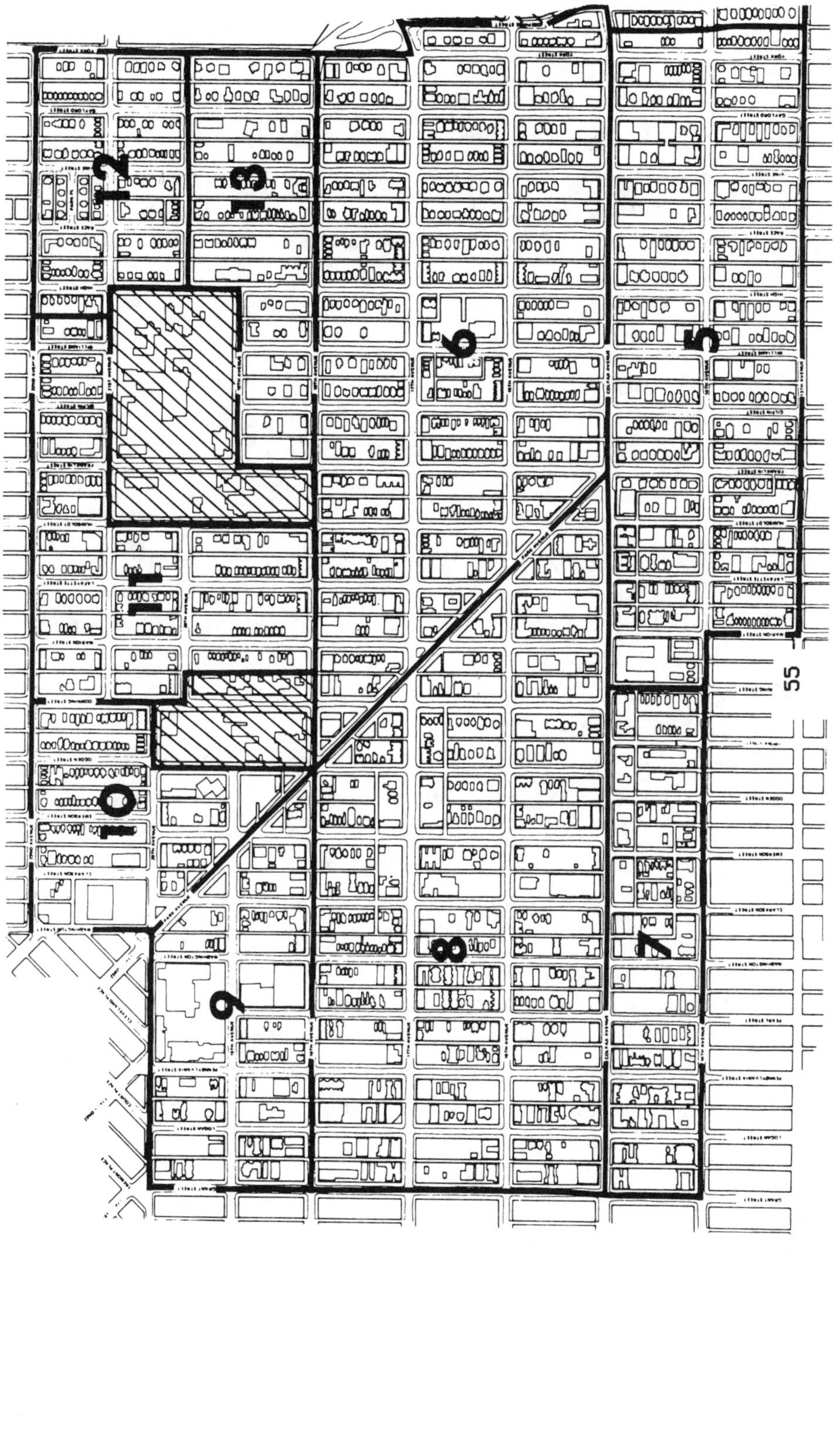

Identifying Issues

With all the above information collected, analyzed, and displayed, it will not take much effort to identify issues around which the remainder of the planning work will revolve; in fact, they may jump right out at you. Examples of how they might be stated are:

- "Northeast corner of the neighborhood is starting to show signs of housing deterioration."
- "Heavy traffic along Maple Street endangers kids walking home from Crowder School."
- "Neighborhood lacks enough small, retail shops to satisfy most day-to-day needs."
- "Historic homes along South Street are vital assets in that they typify what the neighborhood's character is."
- "Population of the neighborhood is aging, and many elderly lack ability to keep up their homes; also services for them are too far away."
- "Many properties are being used in ways that conflict with the present zoning."
- "With rapid population turnover, a sense of community has not been maintained."
- "All parts of neighborhood, except northeast corner, have easy access to public open space."

Notice that the issue statements do not yet imply any specific goal, let alone any proposed action to meet the goal. They are simply rather bland, neutral statements of existing situations, usually stated as problems or at least challenges, about which large numbers of people agree. They may even be statements about positive situations which need support or preservation. Each of them could call forth from the residents varied goal statements and then more varied actions. That part is still to come. These issues typically get identified at some kind of public meeting, after mountains of information have been presented to the attendees. Perhaps a survey had been done, on which respondents also had the chance to identify issues. Whatever means had been used up to this point, at this juncture, all the issues are pulled together and listed in one long list.

The value of identifying these neutrally stated issues is that it may prove easier to get consensus on them than on the goals, which you will be taking up next. If you hop straight from the data to your goals, you are likely to see divisiveness on goals because different residents are in effect defining the issue differently. So, look at the data, then identify issues, then move on to goals. Achieving consensus on the issues should help keep the team together as it moves on to goal setting.

SETTING GOALS

Areas for Goal Setting

The issues state what you want to do something about; the goals state what it is you mean to do, although not yet in detail. Goals may be stated in various ways. One or more goals could be stated, for instance, for each of the categories about which information was collected (e.g., land use, housing, community facilities, etc.). Alternatively, the **PARK** categories could be used:

Preserve (what we have now that is positive).

Add (what we do not have that is positive).

Remove (what we have that is negative).

Keep out (what we do not have that is negative).

Virtually anything that anyone has to say about the neighborhood can fit comfortably into one of those four categories. Still another way to write goals is to prepare some for each of the issues previously identified. Then too, one might wish to formulate goals for geographic subareas of the neighborhood. Any of these approaches will work, or the planning group may wish to combine them and add yet other categories. The important thing is simply to be sure that everything residents want addressed is indeed addressed in some goal statement.

Methods of Stating Goals

Following are examples of typical goal statements for neighborhood planning. Notice each is short, contains only one major thought, gets beyond "apple pie and motherhood," features an action word, and does not specify how it will be met (which comes later).

- "Increase recreational opportunities for youth within the neighborhood."
- "Develop a clear, unified, and unifying image for the neighborhood."
- "Maintain a small scale feel in the eastern end of the neighborhood."
- "Reduce the through traffic on Southern Boulevard."
- "Continue to offer a variety of housing options for varied income groups."

- "Embark on a major street tree-planting effort, especially in areas with substantial numbers of aging and/or diseased trees."
- "Increase the ability of the neighborhood to have its voice heard by local public officials."
- "Upgrade the quality of the middle school, especially with regard to its physical plant."

Participatory Methods of Goal Setting

Perhaps as important as writing clear goals is making sure they represent the neighborhood's residents. That gets us into techniques for participatory goal setting as previously mentioned. A neighborhood planning team can use surveys to get ideas for goals or do the goal setting at a meeting with some special format. The format may be something like:

- Full group brainstorms issues/areas in which members want goals included.
- Small groups each take one or more areas and do a first draft goal statement for each issue.
- Small groups report back to full group, get general endorsement of each statement's sense (not specific wording).
- Writing committee is named to polish up the wording before the next meeting.
- At next meeting, specific statements are presented, reviewed, revised if necessary, and then adopted.

A planning team might use various types of visioning exercises, such as having people write or draw a picture of the neighborhood the way they want it to be five years from now. Or, some kind of budgeting game could be played, where one has a certain number of points to allocate among various proposed goal statements. Some goal statements may take more points to buy than others. After everyone present makes individual decisions, all points allocated are tallied up and that yields a list of top goals. Another technique, in which small groups each prepare various sketch maps, is described in some detail in Appendix C.

PUTTING YOUR PLAN TOGETHER

Recommendations

Now the fun begins: once the goals have been set, it is time to devise policies, strategies, and specific actions to use in pursuing those goals, in addition to preparing maps that show how the neighborhood might look in the future. The recommendations in neighborhood plans usually take the form of *policy statements and maps.* There is a definite progression here from the general to the specific: goals, policies, strategies, specific actions. Goals are broad, sweeping statements about things the planning group would like; policies are general principles to be followed in pursuit of the goals; strategies are more specific methods; specific actions are first steps to take. Let's illustrate:

Goal: Develop a clearer, unified, and unifying image for the neighborhood.

Policy: Adopt by consensus a name, motto, and logo for the neighborhood.

Strategy: Conduct a contest for name, motto, and logo, open to all residents of the neighborhood.

Specific Action: Advertise the contest in various media; solicit gifts from neighborhood merchants for winning entries; create committee to select winning entries.

Goal: Continue to offer a variety of housing options for varied income groups.

Policy: Pursue all available public, private, and nonprofit programs that might be able to provide affordable housing.

Strategy: Select appropriate program and begin process of applying for it.

Specific Action: Create a special task force to explore all programs and report back to the neighborhood organization by (date).

Alternatives

As can be seen in those two examples, each goal requires a series of increasingly specific statements in order to be implemented. For any goal, there are an infinite number of possible ways of reaching it. Clearly, once subjected to close scrutiny, many of those ways will drop out of the running, but it is important to give consideration to several ways of reaching a goal before settling on one. As an example, let's take the goal of "increasing recreational opportunities for youth within the neighborhood." That could be met in various ways:

- Applying for city funds to expand the offerings at the local community center
- Creating a new nonprofit organization which will then raise funds to start a program

- Working with the schools to use those facilities for after-hours programs
- Encouraging private businesses to open more pools, bowling alleys, and other facilities

A neighborhood planning group needs to spend time systematically brainstorming some alternative approaches for each goal. *Brainstorming*, as previously mentioned, is probably the best approach to use, followed by open group discussion about which approach would be best.

Maps

The maps that should be included in the plan, in addition to the many maps that display existing conditions (e.g., land use, zoning, or housing), are ones showing proposed future conditions, that is, the changes the neighborhood wants:

- **Proposed land use** (e.g., some vacant land should be used as a buffering for the industrial area; consolidate retail area to center on the office area as a market).
- **Proposed rezoning** (e.g., the warehouse area, currently zoned for industry, needs to be rezoned for retail activity).
- **Proposed circulation system** (e.g., the heavy through traffic on Southern Boulevard can be partially diverted to the nearby freeway).
- **Proposed housing plan** (e.g., the identification of vacant or inappropriately used sites suitable for new housing).
- **Proposed community facilities** (e.g., a possible site for a senior recreation center would be shown).
- **Proposed urban design plan** (e.g., a gateway to the neighborhood at 8th and Ridge; planting of trees along Southern Boulevard; designation of the old Gilmore House and the Sheedy School as historic landmarks, etc.).

As with the maps of existing conditions, those of proposed changes can be easily done with magic markers, and a simple legend of symbols to indicate various kinds of changes, such as additions, replacements, or eliminations. Examples of maps showing proposed changes can be seen in Figures 13–14 to 13–19.

FIGURING OUT HOW TO IMPLEMENT YOUR PLAN

How Plans Get Implemented

The normal tools that cities use to implement plans are controls over the city's budget for capital investments (usually called the capital improvements plan, or CIP) and controls on land use (such as zoning and other means). City spending on capitol improvements covers such items as streets, sewers, schools, public buildings, and the like. Where the city decides to spend money for sewers, for instance, can shape where new development will occur; how it spends money for housing rehabilitation can heavily influence whether a declining neighborhood can start to come back. Neighbors wishing to get a plan implemented are well advised to learn the city's budgeting process, and when and how citizens can influence it. Land use controls, as the other class to tools for implementing plans, include:

- **Zoning** (which says how a parcel of land may be used).
- **Subdivision regulations** (which dictates how land may be carved up for new developments).
- **Site plan review** (which regulates details in the plans of major developments, such as shopping centers or multifamily complexes).
- **Design review** (which regulates some aspects of the aesthetics of buildings, where such reviews exist).
- **Historic preservation** (which attempts to prevent the loss of architecturally or historically significant structures).

A neighborhood planner can convey to residents the details of how each of these processes works in your particular city. Like the budget, they, too, can be influenced by citizen action.

Gearing a Plan for Implementation

Not all plans stand an equal chance of being implemented, and just because a group of neighborhood residents (and a planner) worked many long hours preparing a plan is no guarantee that it will be implemented. Why plans do not get implemented is partially technical and largely political. This section will cover some of the technical aspects of the plan document itself that can increase the chances of its being implemented.

Figure 3–14. Map of Proposed Land Uses

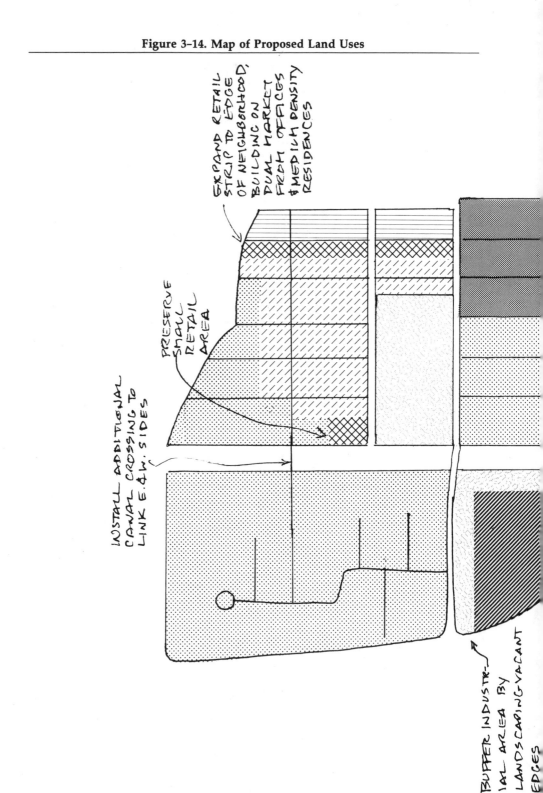

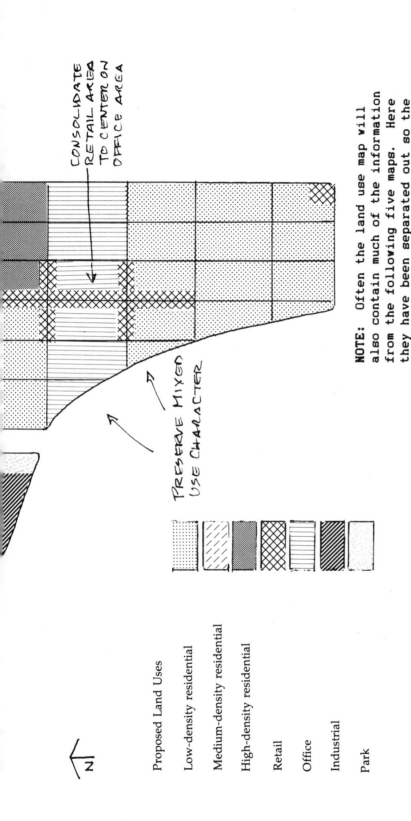

CONSOLIDATE RETAIL AREA TO CENTER ON OFFICE AREA

PRESERVE MIXED USE CHARACTER

NOTE: Often the land use map will also contain much of the information from the following five maps. Here they have been separated out so the reader can more easily see each set of proposed changes.

60

N

Proposed Land Uses

Low-density residential

Medium-density residential

High-density residential

Retail

Office

Industrial

Park

Figure 3-15. Map of Proposed Rezoning

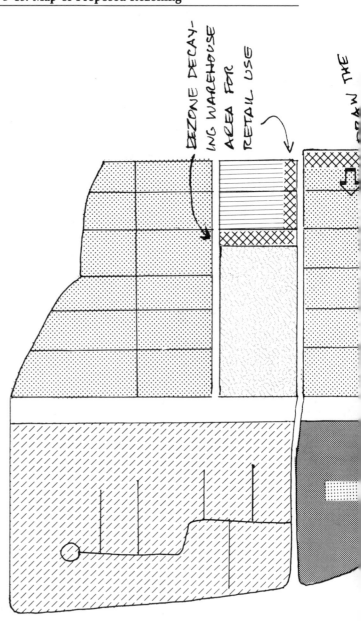

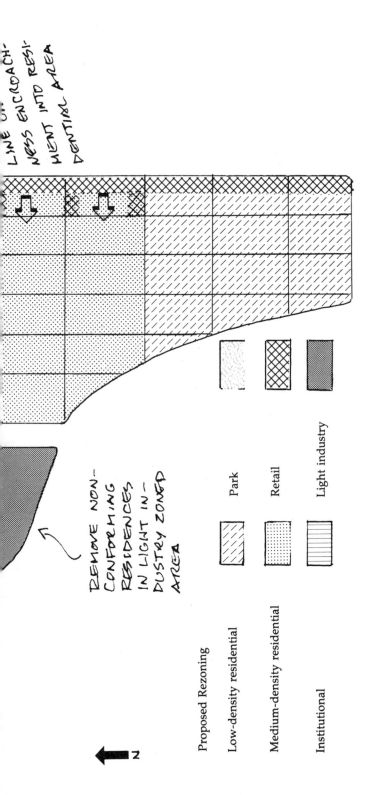

LINE OF BUSINESS ENCROACHMENT INTO RESIDENTIAL AREA

REMOVE NON-CONFORMING RESIDENCES IN LIGHT INDUSTRY ZONED AREA

Proposed Rezoning

Low-density residential

Medium-density residential

Institutional

Park

Retail

Light industry

Figure 3-16. Map of Proposed Circulation Changes

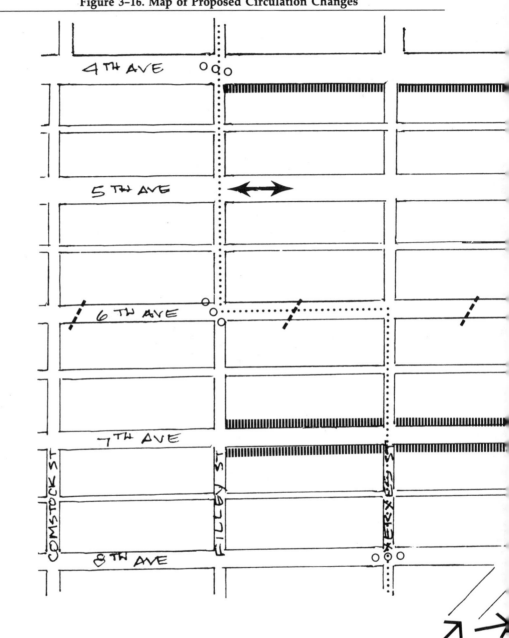

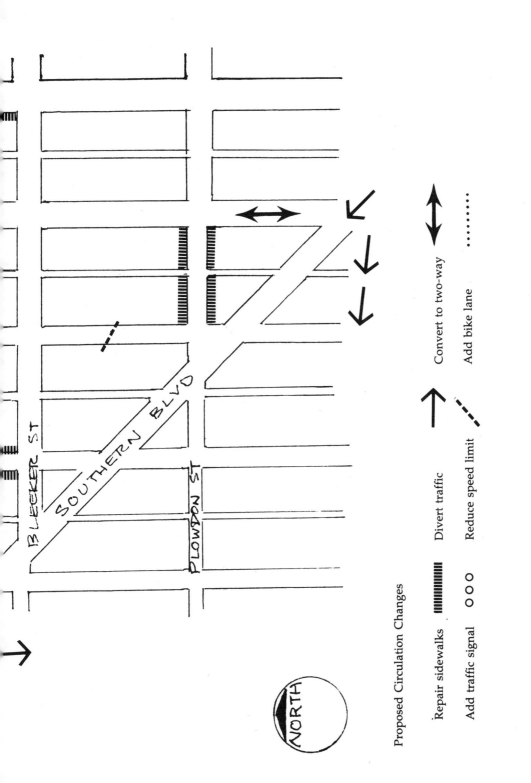

Proposed Circulation Changes

Repair sidewalks   ▮▮▮▮▮▮   Divert traffic

Add traffic signal   O O O   Reduce speed limit

Convert to two-way

Add bike lane

NORTH

Figure 3–17. Map of Proposed Housing Changes

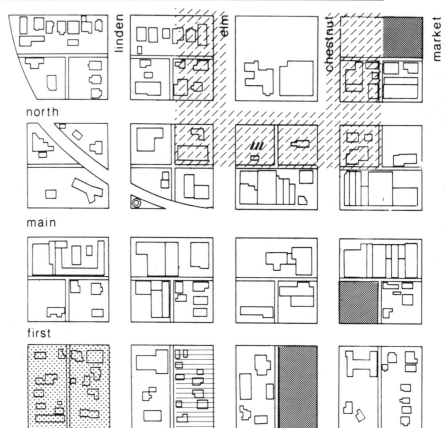

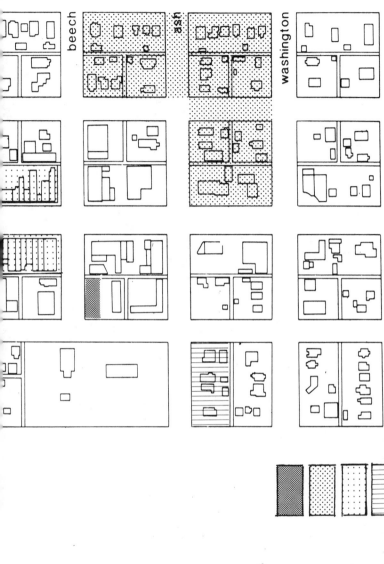

Proposed Housing Changes

Possible in-fill projects

Needs rehab program

Increase density

Downzone (reduce) density

Phase out housing around factory

Figure 3–18. Map of Proposed Community Services and Facilities Changes

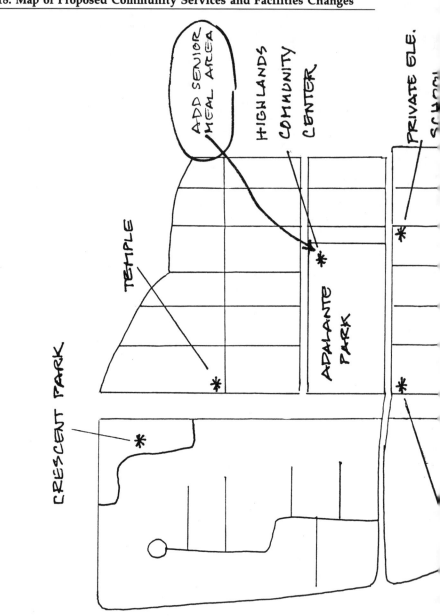

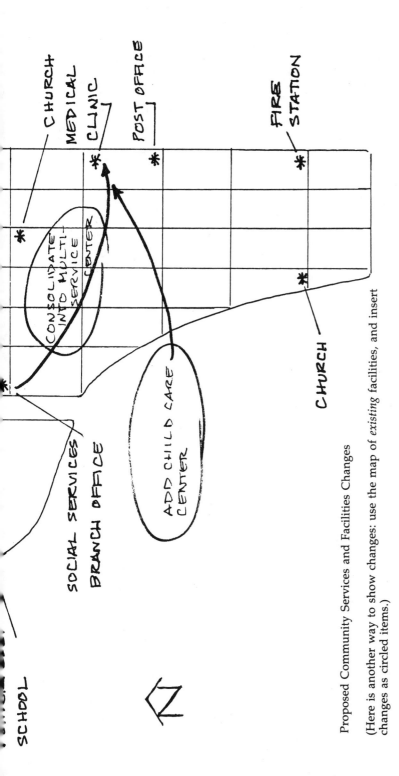

Proposed Community Services and Facilities Changes

(Here is another way to show changes: use the map of *existing* facilities, and insert changes as circled items.)

Figure 3–19. Map of Proposed Urban Design Improvements

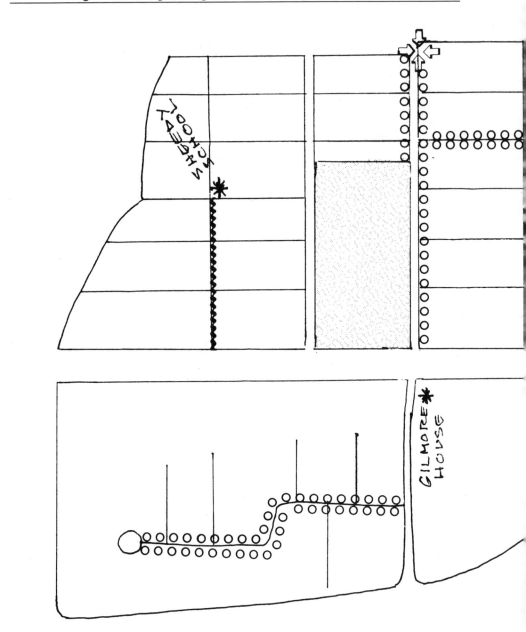

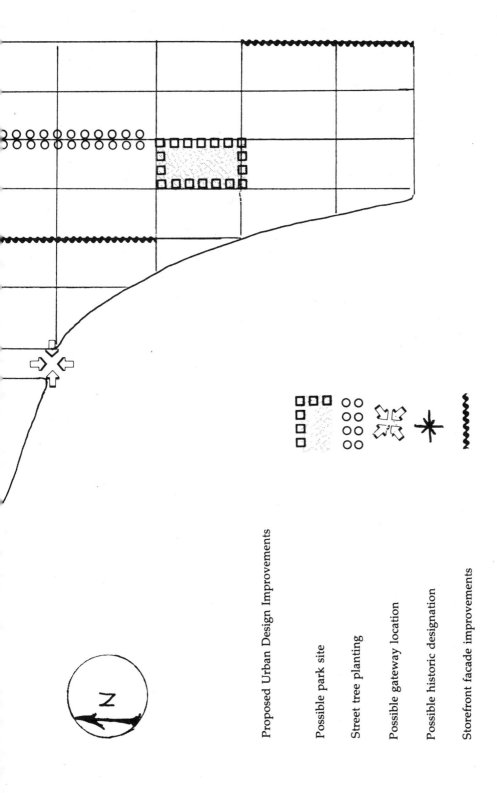

Proposed Urban Design Improvements

Possible park site

Street tree planting

Possible gateway location

Possible historic designation

Storefront facade improvements

First, the language used in making the recommendations can be precise or vague, or somewhere in between. Precisely written recommendations stand a better chance of being acted on; they state things succinctly, specify who needs to do what, and sometimes by when. A recommendation that reads something like "increase the open space in the neighborhood" is vague and does not point to any definitive action by anyone. A stronger recommendation might read something like "the neighborhood organization should work with the city council representative to obtain Community Development Block Grant funds on the next year's funding cycle for purchase of the vacant lot at 4th and Steel for park use."

A second feature of the plan itself that will help in getting it implemented is the presence of priorities and timelines. Let us suppose there are several big ticket items of capital improvements called for in the plan. The city council is not likely to give you all you want right away, if ever. By prioritizing your needs, you help the decisionmakers decide what to address first. Wherever timelines for action can be attached as well, that helps, although it does not commit anyone else to your time table!

Anytime you can attach to a recommendation a cost estimate, you are making decisionmaking easier for others. This third feature cannot always be included because of the difficulties in estimating costs of some changes the neighborhood wants. Many things you want, however, probably have been done elsewhere and costs of those projects can be obtained from the city, from contractors, from designers, and others (an appropriate task for the planner to complete) and used as ball park figures. Many changes you might want might not cost very much, such as changing some traffic patterns or changing some abstract policy. Certainly, cost estimates should be sought for your most important recommendations.

Fourth, decisionmakers often see a plan and react by saying, "Well, that is all well and good, and those are reasonable requests, but where are we supposed to get the money to pay for them?" Anytime you can suggest possible funding sources, you are doing them a favor and maybe winning their favor. This may take some research on the part of the professional planner, but various city offices can help you identify federal funds, state funds, city dollars, foundation assistance, and ideas for local fund-raising. Your Congressional representative and state representative should be called on to help you track down federal and state resources, respectively. Check out the catalog of federal assistance at the public library, along with a directory of foundations in your area. Of course, if you can show the city government that there are other, noncity dollars that can be found, you'll again be making friends.

A fifth tactic that the planning team can take that may help in getting the plan acted upon is to note explicitly in the plan where it is in support of provisions of the current comprehensive plan (or any other plan), and note as well where there are inconsistencies.

Monitoring, Evaluating, and Updating Your Plan

Plans should not be viewed as static documents, but as parts of an on-going process in which citizens remain vigilant about conditions in their neighborhood and continually work to improve them. This means monitoring changes and revising the plan as necessary. Suppose some large store closes down and a whole commercial strip starts to decay in its wake? It is time to pull out the plan, check what you wanted to happen in that particular area, and perhaps rethink that.

If neighborhood residents do not keep on top of the way the plan is being acted on, it is not likely anyone else will. Assuming your neighborhood has a neighborhood organization (it should!!), there might be a special committee that periodically checks what has been done, what still needs doing, what parts of the plan might need revising. It makes sense to write into the plan itself how this process will be done, not that such a provision makes it automatically happen, but it serves as a reminder in writing.

The task of completing a neighborhood plan and that of monitoring conditions in your neighborhood on a regular basis go hand in hand. In many areas, the neighborhood organization actively watches what is going on, and responds to specific problems, whether it be a land use, transportation, housing, social service problem or whatever. The plan can play a useful role as a documentation of existing conditions and as a rationale for your organization's position on the issue. Many is the neighborhood organization that will testify that life is a series of brushfires to be fought. Brushfire-fighting, however, keeps the neighborhood on its toes, strengthens it, and may even inadvertently serve to get some recommendation in the plan implemented as actions are taken in response to immediate crises.

The professional planner can be expected to play a role in assisting the neighborhood with these specific problems. He or she may in fact be the first one to learn of the issue (e.g., a proposed new development, traffic change, public works action, etc.). That information should be passed on to residents immediately, so they can check out the situation and formulate their position. The planner might then be asked to provide yet other information, and should be ready to do that.

In cities with something like a "neighborhood notification ordinance," registered neighborhood organizations are notified in writing as soon as applications for various actions are filed, such as for rezoning, variances, street or alley closures, or liquor license applications. This early warning system lets residents know something has been proposed, and usually in time enough for them to investigate, take a stance, and intervene in the process.

Yet, another device some organizations use is to line up volunteers who monitor their own block systematically and regularly. Such "adopt-a-block" systems keep residents in touch with changes and allow the organization to address problems proactively, before they get out of hand. If vigilanteeism in its negative connotation can be avoided, there is something very healthy in residents taking on themselves the responsibility for detecting problems rather than having an impersonal inspector from the city breathing down someone's throat.

So, the neighborhood that is everwatchful, that is, receives and reads its mail from the city, stays in close contact with its neighborhood planner, and attends to what is going on, will be in a superior position when it comes to monitoring and updating its plan. To rephrase the point made earlier: the long-term task of planning and the short-term task of responding to immediate problems reinforce one another.

4

After the Planning

PREPARING THE FINAL DOCUMENT

Contents of the Document

All the parts of the plan have been described earlier, along with guidance about how to do each step. This section will discuss how to put them all together into a pretty package. To review: the contents should include:

Executive Summary: a 3-5 page summary of the whole document, written for the busy executive who won't read the whole thing! (strictly narrative plus one or two maps)

Table of Contents

Introduction (mostly narrative, maybe a chart of the process used)
  Purpose: why this plan has been done and any unique circumstances that provided the impetus
  Scope of the plan: what it is and what it is not
  Planning process used, participants involved, roles played
  Map showing the neighborhood outlined within a larger city map

Description of Existing Conditions (narrative, maps, tables, etc.)
  Natural environmental features
  · Existing land use
  Zoning
  Circulation
  Utilities
  Housing
  Community facilities and services
  Urban design features

General physical conditions
History
Demography
Social analysis
Economic base
Analysis of Situation and Identification of Issues (narrative, maps, tables, etc.)
Goals (narrative)
Possibly categorized and ranked
Long-term and short-term
Recommendations (mostly narrative, some maps or sketches)
Policies
Strategies
Specific actions
Implementation Steps (narrative)
Responsibilities
Timelines
Provisions for monitoring, evaluating, updating
Conclusions (narrative)
Appendix (a place to add supporting materials that you do not want interrupting the flow of the main text)
How-to's: materials you may have found that detail how some recommendation can be implemented, or the story of how some other neighborhood did what you want to do
Agencies, programs, contact persons to assist in plan implementation
Old maps
Lengthy data

Packaging the Document

Producing the physical document should not be just an afterthought, but the result of careful deliberation. The layout of the document should be attractive in the sense of attention-getting, creative without being cute, and informative. Give consideration to a map or a photograph or a sketch of the neighborhood on the cover. Think through whether it will be on 8 1/2″ x 11″ paper printed as this page is or turned sideways: the shape of your neighborhood might lend itself to the sideways arrangement. Some city planning offices print up neighborhood plans as large posters, combining text, photographs, maps, and so on. These can be attention getting, as long as they also communicate clearly and do not lose the reader. Give some consideration to colored, heavy stock paper as dividers between sections or add plastic tabs to mark each section. This is where your working relationship with the local printer gets tested: What kind of discount or free work can you obtain?

How many copies of the document to prepare depends largely on your budget. Certainly all the key people in the neighborhood and the neighborhood planner who worked on it should receive copies, as well as other neighborhood leaders who may not have been involved. Then there are public officials: city council members and mayor, planning department staff and commissioners, other helpful officials with whom you worked, and the press. The planning office may have a policy about how many copies of plans they normally run. If a neighborhood planner has been involved in the preparation of your plan, the planning office should foot the bill for the printing; if residents did all the work, the planning office might still be talked into picking up the printing cost. After all, look at all the money you saved them by your doing the work!

You may wish to take the executive summary and a few key maps/ tables/charts, as well as any other pertinent data and bind those together as a short summary version, which can be printed in larger quantities for wider distribution.

WINNING SUPPORT FOR AND APPROVAL OF YOUR PLAN

Getting the Neighborhood Behind the Plan

For a neighborhood plan to have legal status in most cities, it needs to be adopted by both the planning commission or board and the city council. (In some communities, those two bodies may be one and the same.) Before you even approach those bodies, *it is crucial that the neighborhood really be behind it.* Of course, if you have had decent involvement through the planning process itself and have had public presentations of early drafts of the plan, you are half-way home (although there may well be some who were involved and still oppose the plan fully or in part). There are a number of other steps you can also take to increase neighborhood support; your group may come up with still others:

Disseminate the plan (or a concise summary of it) widely within the neighborhood and the city:

residents

public officials

neighborhood institutions
the media.

Present the plan before any willing audience. (Be sure a few people are well rehearsed to present it clearly).

Prepare or help reporters to prepare articles about the plan for neighborhood and citywide newspapers.

Post flyers around the neighborhood about the plan's completion, the availability of copies of the summary, and the public hearings on it.

Obtain letters of endorsement of the plan from residents, organizations, businesses, and neighborhood institutions.

Do not forget to celebrate its completion or unveiling!

Winning Support from Public Officials

Then, having built a neighborhood consensus for the plan, you can start on the public officials. Again, if you have kept them informed with progress reports all along the way, you have part of the job done. But take every opportunity now to present it to the key officials before officially submitting it to the planning commission. If the plan has been prepared by residents on their own, it should be presented to the planning staff first: It would be impolite to bypass them. In fact, the staff may be the best parties to present it to the commission. Or at the least they need to endorse your presentation.

Once it is scheduled for a public hearing before either the planning commission and/or the city council, you will need to rally the troops to be at those hearings and voice their support of the plan. Speakers are necessary, but warm bodies, too shy to testify, are also helpful at public hearings: a speaker, for instance, can ask everyone in the audience who supports the plan to stand. The presentations at these public hearings should be carefully orchestrated, that is, different speakers each focus on special aspects of the plan, rather than having 23 people all get up and say the same thing. City council members always appreciate brevity and nonrepetition. Making the public hearing a real occasion can help too: such as organizing a caravan of vehicles going down to city hall, getting the media to cover it, having a rally beforehand. But do not embarrass or attack city council, or they may cloud up and rain all over you!

Some of the specific tasks to accomplish at this juncture are:

Meet informally with your city council representative to answer questions and elicit support in advance of any hearing.

Do the same with planning office staff and commissioners.

Ascertain the dates of the hearings before the planning commission and the council.

Advertise those events and organize folks to attend them.

Study the format and rules for the hearing and orchestrate your group's testimony accordingly.

Provide transportation to the hearings, if necessary.

Stage a caravan or other hoopla to go along with those events.

WATCHING OVER PLAN IMPLEMENTATION

As mentioned earlier, the neighborhood has to take the lead in getting a neighborhood plan put into action. You should have a formal mechanism to do that and to keep on top of things. That formal group might consider creating some standard for what implementation means (when exactly you can check off a recommendation as having been accomplished), set up a schedule of activities for themselves and others to do, and arrange for regular feedback to the rest of the neighborhood on what is happening. The full neighborhood, of course, would be the ones to act on that feedback about progress or the lack thereof.

Finally, do not expect the city council to fulfill all the requests you have included in the plan. As you develop goals, policies, strategies, and action agendas, look for and identify projects the neighborhood can do on its own. While your planning team may seem insufficient in size and energy to accomplish all that you want, remember that you have a whole neighborhood full of people to help you, if you can help them organize and act on things that they want. In any neighborhood, there are usually people who like to plan things and others who like to do things. (Both types are needed, of course.) If you start by recruiting people for fun work projects, you will be demonstrating that community improvement activities can be both productive and enjoyable. Periodic visible projects will show city officials that the neighborhood is committed and therefore deserving of support. More importantly, it will help you and your neighbors create the kind of caring, sharing community in which most of us want to live. Do not forget the planner who may have worked with you: do not lose contact with that person just because the document has been published. Tactfully exploit his or her connection to city hall.

The other thing the planning team can do about implementation is to take the initiative and search out developers or others who might like to do a project that meets their needs while implementing some piece of the plan. Neighborhood folks, of necessity, spend much time reacting to others' proposals and initiatives . . . and get a bad rap for being reactive or reactionary. Turn that process on its head: once you know what you want for the neighborhood, go out and find someone who might want much the same thing. This could, of course, necessitate some negotiation and compromise between the neighborhood desires and those of the developer, but would it not be nice for a change to be the ones dealing the cards?

Appendix A

Computers in Neighborhood Planning

With the increasingly wide availability of computers both in planning offices and in homes, it would be a shame not to use them in neighborhood planning if they can be helpful. That qualifier *if* is important. One needs to be sure that the technology, though second nature to many people today, does not intimidate some people and thus become a barrier. In addition, there is often a temptation to let one's methods lead one by the nose, meaning here, that the needs and style of the computer starts to dictate what information shall be collected, how it shall be analyzed, and how it shall be presented. At least as seductive is the tendency to think (incorrectly so) that the computer can make for you the tough decision your planning team is reluctant to make!

With those notes of caution, let us turn to a brief consideration of some software that is available to the planner, be that the professional or the citizen. The reader should, however, recognize that any information about computer technology and accompanying software can change dramatically in a manner of months as new developments keep expanding our capabilities. It would be far beyond the scope of this guide to identify, describe, and evaluate specific software packages or to describe in any detail how to use them. However, we can offer thumbnail sketches of various categories of software and how they might be used in neighborhood planning. Where possible, one or two specific, widely used software packages will be identified. The American Planning Association's Software Distribution Service, housed at the University of Akron, can make available inexpensive software packages to do many of the tasks described below.

Word Processing. Probably the most familiar use of the computer is word processing. Word processing certainly can be useful in the preparing of any written materials used during planning work and in preparing the final report. The key feature of word processing that would be helpful here is the easy ability to edit (change) what has been written as the planning team reviews a document and decides to change it. Examples: *WordPerfect, Microsoft Word.*

Desktop Publishing and Graphics. The desktop publishing family of software allows one to lay out written and graphic materials in an infinite number of interesting ways. Suppose, for instance, a planning team decided to print up its final report in an eye-catching format, to look like a daily newspaper, with multiple columns, photos, different sizes and styles of headlines, and so forth. Desktop publishing software allows one to do that and many other layout tasks that formerly could be done only by a professional printing shop. Related to desktop publishing are graphic software packages that allow information, such as statistical data, to be portrayed in all manner of charts and graphs. These can spice up a report, if one is getting tired of pages and pages of tables that all look alike after a while. Examples: *First Publisher, Harvard Graphics.*

Project Scheduling. There are a number of programs on the market that allow

107

one to take a complex project, such as planning and constructing a building, and lay it out step by step. Among the items that can be shown are which tasks have to proceed which other ones, how effectively resources are being used, where time is being wasted, and what is the quickest way to get the job done. Most neighborhood planning efforts, as projects, are probably not complex enough to warrant scheduling them in this manner, although it might be interesting to plot out the implementation of a plan in this manner. Examples: *MacProject II, Time Line, ViewPoint.*

Databases and Database Searches. These two ideas can be linked together. By databases I mean existing sources of information, such as U.S. Census data, that are now available on disks for anyone to purchase. The U.S. government and several commercial companies make available census information that is more concise than fat printed reports, less costly to purchase, allows additional analysis, and can be tied into other software, such as your word processing system. Software packages are available that will make projections on the population, given certain birth rates, death rates, and so on. While most census information at the neighborhood level is not yet available on disks, one can obtain some small-area statistics. It is likely that in the future, more data will be available. Examples: *U.S. Bureau of the Census, Strategic Locations Planning, CACI.*

Database searches refer to the ability to call up on one's personal computer (through a modem, for example) the national services that maintain massive amounts of categorized information about every topic under the sun. One pays a fee to subscribe to such a service and then a small fee each time you call up for some information. If a neighborhood planning group is facing some issue the local planning office has not yet addressed, for example, it might be possible to obtain information, through a database search, about some other communities that have faced the issue. This could be very useful for expanding the group's mental horizons.

The computer user with a modem can also, of course, call up another specific person's computer in a system known as electronic mail and ask that person for certain information. Unlike the telephone, electronic mail does not require the other party be there when the call is placed: the message can be left at any time.

Spreadsheets. Spreadsheets are grids of information, such as land use characteristics of each block in a neighborhood. With a spreadsheet, one can store a vast amount of information, manipulate it, and then print it out. The manipulation capability allows one to pose "what-if" questions, where new decisions are proposed, and the program will show what effects it would have on other parts of the neighborhood. In neighborhood planning, this could greatly facilitate the exploration of alternative proposal. Example: *Lotus 1-2-3, Quattropro, Excel.*

Database Management. In addition to using other people's databases, planning teams will likely generate huge amounts of their own information. This can be placed within databases you create. Database management programs allow quick calculations of all sorts on the data entered into one's database. Examples: *dBASE, R:BASE.*

Statistical Analysis. In the planning process, often one collects much statistical information, which requires some analysis. Suppose, for instance, a household survey is conducted, where 200 households are each asked 50 different questions; that's 10,000 pieces of information! We now have software packages that can do the number crunching and help determine what groups in the neighborhood have what kinds of outlooks. Examples: *SPSSx, SAS, dBASE.*

Thematic Mapping and Geographic Information Systems. Thematic maps are computer generated maps that would show, for example, the housing density of different parts of the neighborhood by various shadings. The land use map that uses different colors for each land use could also be cranked out by the computer, either with shadings or colors (if one has a printer that can do that).

Geographic information systems (GIS) take thematic mapping one—or several steps—farther, allowing one to produce maps that show how several different factors (e.g., housing density, cost, and distance from the downtown) are related to one another. GIS is akin to crossing a computer-generated map with a database, so that what you get is a map with very rich information displayed on it. As events occur, such as rezoning of a parcel of land, that new information can be entered easily and its effects shown. Examples: *ESRI, Intergraph, GeoVision.*

Simulation. Sometimes in neighborhood planning one would like to act out a pretend situation: "What would the neighborhood be like if we were to do . . . ?" Simulation packages allow users to do things like create make-believe cities. Then all those participating play out their roles (make their moves), creating new situations, which then become the basis for the next round of moves, and so on. At this point, there are packages for simulating cities; perhaps soon, there will be neighborhood-scaled ones. Example: *SimCity.*

Computer-Aided Design and Drafting. Somewhat like word processing, computer-aided design and drafting (CAD) systems allow one to draw (instead of write) something, store it, and then change it as often as one likes. In addition, one can play with the drawing, in the sense of imposing "what-if" conditions on it and watching what are the consequences. With CAD, one can, for example, draw a picture of a housing development on a vacant parcel of land in the neighborhood, then rotate the picture to see what it might look like from all four sides. CAD can also be used to produce sketches or maps for the final plan document. Examples: *AutoCAD, CADKEY, Generic CADD.*

Appendix B

Citizen Survey

Part I: Residency and Housing

First, we are interested in knowing how you feel about housing in Simla.

1. What is your present housing situation? (Circle one)

   1 - rent   2 - own

2. In what type of housing do you live? (Circle one)

   1 - single family house   4 - boarding house or room
   2 - duplex   5 - apartment
   3 - mobile home   6 - other (specify) _____

3. How satisfied are you with your present home? (Circle one)

   1 - very satisfied   3 - dissatisfied
   2 - satisfied   4 - very dissatisfied

4. What types of new housing do you think should be built in Simla? (Circle no more than 2 numbers)

   1 - none   5 - townhouses/condominiums
   2 - low income housing complex   6 - apartments
   3 - single family houses   7 - all of the above
   4 - mobile home parks   8 - other (specify) _____

5. How would you rate the overall housing stock in Simla? (Circle one)

   1 - very adequate   3 - inadequate
   2 - adequate   4 - very inadequate

6. Which of the following statements best reflects your feelings about future location of residential mobile homes in Simla? (Circle one)

   1 - should be allowed in any area of town
   2 - should be allowed to locate in residential areas only
   3 - should be allowed in mobile home parks only
   4 - no additional mobile homes should be allowed in Simla

7. If your housing situation is satisfactory to you, do you feel that your home and its condition should be of any concern to other townspeople? (Circle one)

   1 - yes   2 - no   3 - uncertain

8. If another person's house seems substandard to you, do you feel that you have a responsibility for correcting the situation (by notifying the owners or the proper town authorities)?

   1 - yes   2 - no   3 - uncertain

9. What is your monthly payment for housing, "rent or mortgage"?

   $ _____

10. Should more than one mobile home dwelling be allowed on a residential lot in Simla?

1 - yes   2 - no   3 - unsure

Part II: Community Living

Next, we would like to know some of your thoughts and ideas about life in Simla.

1. What are the two best aspects of day-to-day life in Simla for you?

    1. _____

    2. _____

2. What are the major disadvantages, if any, of living in Simla?

    _____

    _____

3. How satisfied are you with the quality of life in Simla? (Circle one)

    1 - very satisfied   4 - dissatisfied
    2 - satisfied   5 - very dissatisfied
    3 - neutral

4. Which one of the following words best describes the way you feel about your life in Simla? (Circle one)

    1 - happy   5 - dull
    2 - frustrated   6 - hurried
    3 - lonely   7 - anxious
    4 - peaceful   8 - fulfilled
                                          9 - fair to middling

5. Please circle the response that best describes your feeling about each of the following statements:

    a. the future of this town looks bright

       1 - strongly agree   4 - disagree
       2 - agree   5 - strongly disagree
       3 - neutral

    b. people won't work together to get things done for this town

       1 - strongly agree   4 - disagree
       2 - agree   5 - strongly disagree
       3 - neutral

    c. this town has good leaders

       1 - strongly agree   4 - disagree
       2 - agree   5 - strongly disagree
       3 - neutral

    d. residents of this town continually look for new solutions to problems rather than being satisfied with things as they are

       1 - strongly agree   4 - disagree
       2 - agree   5 - strongly disagree
       3 - neutral

6. What is the major change, if any, that you have seen occur in Simla over the past five years? _____

_____

7. What is the one major improvement that would make living in Simla better for you?_____

_____

8. What is the quality about Simla that you most want to preserve? _____

_____

Part III: Community Facilities and Services

We are also interested in how you view the facilities and services available to you in Simla.

1. How would you rate the following aspects of the school system?

	very satisfied	satisfied	unsure	dissatisfied	very dissatisfied
1. education programs	1	2	3	4	5
2. school facilities	1	2	3	4	5
3. administration	1	2	3	4	5
4. other (specify)	1	2	3	4	5

2. If the school facility were made available for "after-school" use by community groups, would you and your family or group be likely to use it? (Circle one)

1 - yes   2 - no   3 - unsure

3. What one major improvement would you like to see made in the public school district in the next year?_____

_____

4. How important are each of the following Simla concerns, if any, to you? (Circle one answer for each question.)

	very important	somewhat important	not important
1. enactment of building codes	1	2	3
2. land use planning	1	2	3
3. enactment of zoning codes	1	2	3
4. park improvements	1	2	3
5. enactment of animal control codes	1	2	3
6. recreation programs	1	2	3
7. environmental protection	1	2	3
8. economic development	1	2	3
9. water quality	1	2	3

10. citizen participation in local
   planning   1   2   3
11. other (specify) _____   1   2   3

5. Of those you have marked as "very important" in Question 4 above, list your priority (using the numbers in the left column) that local government should work on during the next year.

   Your first priority: _____
   Your second priority: _____
   Your third priority: _____

6. Rate the adequacy of the following community services and facilities in Simla: (Circle one answer for each category.)

		Excellent	Adequate	In Need of Improvement	Non-Existent	Don't Know
1.	street maintenance	1	2	3	4	5
2.	sidewalks	1	2	3	4	5
3.	street lights	1	2	3	4	5
4.	curbs and gutters	1	2	3	4	5
5.	drainage	1	2	3	4	5
6.	police protection	1	2	3	4	5
7.	speed control	1	2	3	4	5
8.	traffic control	1	2	3	4	5
9.	fire protection	1	2	3	4	5
10.	animal control	1	2	3	4	5
11.	water service	1	2	3	4	5
12.	snow removal	1	2	3	4	5
13.	phone service	1	2	3	4	5
14.	gas/electric service	1	2	3	4	5
15.	health service	1	2	3	4	5
16.	recreation facilities	1	2	3	4	5
17.	parks	1	2	3	4	5
18.	entertainment facilities	1	2	3	4	5
19.	day care centers	1	2	3	4	5
20.	community meetings	1	2	3	4	5
21.	community meeting space	1	2	3	4	5
22.	other (specify) _____	1	2	3	4	5

7. Of the services and facilities above that you marked (in need of improvement or nonexistent) which three (3) should be given the highest priority by your local government? (Use the number from left column above.)

   1. _____ 2. _____ 3. _____

8. Do you feel strongly enough about the services or facilities you marked on Question 5, that you would want *local funds spent* for improving or obtaining them? (Circle one)

    1 - yes   3 - uncertain
    2 - no   4 - other (specify)

Part IV: Land Use Planning

Following are questions concerning your opinion about the future planning and development of Simla.

1. In your opinion, what should be the *upper limit* of the population in Simla? (Circle one)

    1 - under 500 (approximately the present population)
    2 - 600–1,000
    3 - 1,001–1,500
    4 - 1,501–2,000
    5 - over 2,000

2. Which of the following statements would you *most* like to see the town of Simla characterized as ten years from now? (Circle one)

    1 - small agricultural community (sort of as-is)
    2 - bedroom community to Colorado Springs
    3 - retirement community
    4 - relatively self-sufficient community with some industry
    5 - other (specify) _____

3. There is increasing pressure on local government officials to examine the community planning process and land use controls such as zoning, easements, and other regulations to influence the development and use of privately owned land. Please circle the category which *best* reflects how you feel about each of the following statements.

	Strongly Agree	Agree	Disagree	Strongly Disagree
1. No one has the right to tell land-owners what they can and cannot do with their own land	1	2	3	4
2. Land use controls are very useful in achieving orderly growth of a town	1	2	3	4
3. Land use controls are a poor means of protecting natural resources	1	2	3	4
4. Land use controls are a poor means of protecting natural resources	1	2	3	4
5. We need more land use controls in town	1	2	3	4
6. Land use controls will make the town a better place to live	1	2	3	4

7. Land use controls would reduce
   conflict between land owners and
   the public   1   2   3   4
8. Land use controls will increase the
   value of my property   1   2   3   4
9. Most people will be harmed by land
   use controls   1   2   3   4

4. Do you *favor the development* of a master land use plan to guide the future development of Simla? (Circle one)

   1 - yes   2 - no   3 - unsure

5. Would you be *in favor* of the enactment of zoning ordinances in the town of Simla? (Circle one)

   1 - yes   2 - no   3 - unsure

6. If Simla were to develop zoning regulations, which best describes your feelings on how the regulations should be developed? (Circle one)

   1 - no zoning regulations are needed
   2 - very strict, with specific land use controls
   3 - mildly strict, leaving some flexibility
   4 - loose, leaving lots of flexibility

7. Which of the following should Simla town government consider doing in regard to the issue of growth or no-growth? (Circle one)

   1 - develop policies to prevent growth in Simla
   2 - develop policies to guide the slow growth of Simla
   3 - develop policies to promote growth in Simla
   4 - neither encourage nor discourage growth in Simla
   5 - other (specify) _____

8. If growth is to occur, do you feel it is the responsibility of the taxpayer or the developer to take on the burden of paying for growth related costs such as utility extensions (water, sewage, etc., and utility plant improvements)? (Circle one)

   1 - taxpayer   3 - taxpayers and developers
   2 - developer   4 - other (specify) _____

9. Regarding the annexation of land to the town, which of the following statements do you agree with most closely? (Circle one)

   1 - Simla should not annex any new land in the near future
   2 - Simla should annex new land only under strict regulations
   3 - Simla should be allowed to annex new land without any strict regulations

Part V: Economic Conditions

We are interested in how you view the existing and future economic prospects of Simla.

1. What percent of your family purchases are made in Simla? (Circle one)

1 - less than 5%	4 - 16–25%
2 - 5–10%	5 - 26–50%
3 - 11–15%	6 - above 50%

2. Where do you and your family most frequently obtain the following goods and services? (Circle one number for each line.)

Services

	Simla	Colorado Springs	Denver Metro	
beauty shop	1	2	3	4
barber shop	1	2	3	4
drycleaning	1	2	3	4
laundry	1	2	3	4
medical and dental	1	2	3	4
banking	1	2	3	4
restaurant (eating out)	1	2	3	4
auto repair	1	2	3	4
construction services	1	2	3	4
legal services	1	2	3	4
entertainment	1	2	3	4

Goods

	Simla	Colorado Springs	Denver Metro	
grocery	1	2	3	4
drugs/medicine	1	2	3	4
clothing	1	2	3	4
hardware	1	2	3	4
alcoholic beverages	1	2	3	4
gasoline	1	2	3	4
appliances	1	2	3	4
furniture	1	2	3	4
auto parts	1	2	3	4
farm and ranch supplies	1	2	3	4

3. From the above list or other, what three types of retail shops or services do you think are most needed in Simla?

1 - _____ 2 - _____ 3 - _____

4. Which of the following land uses should Simla encourage? (Circle no more than 3 numbers.)

1 - commercial/retail   6 - mobile homes
2 - light industry   7 - professional/technical offices
3 - single family residential   8 - none
4 - multifamily residential   9 - other (specify) _____
5 - senior citizen housing

5. Would you be in favor of the town government providing financial incentives to attract additional industry to Simla? (Circle one.)

   1 - yes   2 - no   3 - unsure

6. Which of the following statements best represents your desires for the way that growth and development in Simla should be guided in the future? (Check only one.)

   _____ We should place an emphasis on improving community services and facilities in order to maintain and improve Simla as an excellent place to reside.

   _____ We should place an emphasis on expanding the economic base in order to provide additional employment opportunities in Simla.

7. Would you be in favor of community efforts to increase economic growth in Simla?

   1 - yes   2 - no   3 - unsure

   If yes, do you believe it should be a: (Circle one.)

   1 - significant effort
   2 - moderate effort
   3 - minimum effort

Part VI: Recreation

Now, a few questions about recreational needs.

1. Please circle any of the following recreation programs or facilities that you and your family regularly use in Simla?

   1 - town park
   2 - town hall
   3 - ball fields

2. What recreation programs or facilities do you and your family regularly use outside of town?

   1. _____   2. _____   3. _____

3. How would you rate existing recreation programs and/or opportunities in the town of Simla? (Circle one)

   1 - good   2 - adequate   3 - poor   4 - don't know

4. Do you think that the following groups have sufficient recreational opportunities in the town of Simla?

Group	Yes	No	No Opinion
1. children	1	2	3
2. teens	1	2	3
3. adults	1	2	3
4. seniors	1	2	3
5. families	1	2	3

5. What one major recreation improvement would you like to see made in Simla during the next year? _____

_____

6. Should the town government assume more responsibility for public recreation programs or facilities in Simla? (Circle one)

    1 - yes   2 - no   3 - unsure

Part VII: You and Your Family

These last few questions are about you and your family. They are very important in helping to interpret the previous information.

1. How long have you lived in or expect to live in Simla? (Write in appropriate number.)

    Lived in Simla _____ years

    Expect to live in Simla _____ years.

2. Sex of respondent: (Circle one.)

    1 - female   2 - male

3. What is your ethnic background? (Circle one)

    1 - Anglo   4 - Asian American
    2 - Hispanic   5 - American Indian
    3 - Black   6 - Other (specify) _____

4. What is your age and your spouse's? (Circle one)

You	Spouse
1 - Under 24 years	- 1
2 - 25 to 34 years	- 2
3 - 35 to 44 years	- 3
4 - 45 to 54 years	- 4
5 - 55 to 59 years	- 5
6 - 60 to 64 years	- 6
7 - 65 and older	- 7

5. Mark the highest level of education you and your spouse have completed. (Circle each column if applicable.)

You	Spouse
1 - junior high (8th grade or less)	- 1
2 - some high school	- 2
3 - high school graduate or GED	- 3
4 - some college	- 4
5 - four-year college graduate	- 5
6 - graduate level work	- 6
7 - graduate degree	- 7

6. What is your marital status? (Circle one.)

1 - never married   4 - separated
2 - now married   5 - widowed
3 - divorced   6 - other (specify) _____

7. In the box below, please indicate the number of males and females in your household in each of the age categories, including yourself.

Age Categories	Male	Female
Under 6 years		
6–11 years		
12–17 years		
18–25 years		
26—39 years		
40—65 years		
Over 65 years		

8. Which of the following categories best describes your or your spouse's (if applicable) present occupation?

You   Spouse

1 - teacher   - 1
2 - professional/technical (doctor, lawyer, etc.)   - 2
3 - farm owner or manager   - 3
4 - owner, proprietor, official, manager (other than farm) - 4
5 - clerical   - 5
6 - sales   - 6
7 - foreman/skilled craftsman   - 7
8 - machine operator   - 8
9 - private household worker   - 9
10 - other service worker (waiter, custodian, etc.)   -10
11 - farm laborer   - 11
12 - laborer   - 12
13 - student   - 13
14 - homemaker   - 14
15 - retired   - 15
16 - unemployed   - 16
17 - disabled/physically unable to work   - 17
18 - other (specify) _____   - 18

9. How many members of your household are wage earners? _____

10. Where (name the town) do you or your spouse work?

Male _____   Female _____

11. What is your family's primary and secondary source of income? (Circle one for each.)

	Primary	Secondary
salary (monthly or yearly)	1	1
wage (hourly and/or tips)	2	2
self-employed	3	3
social security	4	4
public assistance	5	5
independent income (rents, interests, stocks, etc.)	6	6

12. Which category best fits your total family income last year? (Circle one)

1 - less than $5,000
2 - $5,000–$9,999
3 - $10,000–$14,999
4 - $15,000–$19,999
5 - $20,000–$29,999
6 - $30,000–$39,999
7 - $40,000–$49,999
8 - above $50,000

THANK YOU FOR COMPLETING THE QUESTIONNAIRE.

Source: Simla, Colorado, Master Plan (1989)

PALMER LAKE

CITIZENS
WORKSHOP

What are Palmer Lake's assets? What are Palmer Lake's problems? What can be done to make Palmer Lake a more desirable community? How can the local economy be strengthened? Which way should the town council be moving in solving them? These questions can best be answered through a creative partnership between town council, planning commission, economic development task force, and those who have a stake in the community because they operate a business in town, live in town, own property or rely on the community for services. This workshop has been designed to form such a partnership. The intent of this workshop is to assist the citizens of Palmer Lake develop a road map of how to build on existing community assets and correct potential community problems to ensure a strong local economy.

The workshop is designed to allow Palmer Lake citizens to express their ideas about what the town could be, how improvements could be made, and how town policies could change. Below is an outline of how we plan to proceed.

COLLECTING IDEAS: 7:10–8:30 pm

The purpose of tonight's exercise is to get lots of ideas about the community out in the open. We will briefly meet together then break up into small groups. We would hope that people sit with their friends or with other people most like themselves: people operating businesses, government representatives, home-owners, newcomers, old time residents, owners of investment property or people with special interests. Each group will be equipped with maps and markers for making poster-maps of their findings.

Introductions, if necessary, are the first thing to do when each group meets. Next, start on the poster maps. We have provided each group with four base maps of the town. There are four mapping exercises for recording your ideas. Do not forget to come up with a name for your group and include it on each map.

CROWLEY COUNTY GOAL IDENTIFICATION (MAPPING) EXERCISE

I. Explain the purpose of the exercise and its agenda.
    A. Give examples from the Palmer Lake exercise
    B. Ask for questions

II. Be sure that all maps have titles and groups have names (all maps will show all four major communities and the county)
    A. Good/bad (plus where everyone lives)
    B. Ideal (if money no object)
    C. Action (what can be done)

III. Start with four tables, hopefully with 6–10 per table, and ideally eight. Each table should have butcher paper, name tags, maps, red and green magic markers, dots for voting, and eight chairs. Monitor the signup sheet and as we reach 32, 40, 48, etc., set up more tables.

IV.   Facilitator responsibilities include:
   A. Group introductions and asking where people are from—put home locations on map
   B. Name group
   C. Put group's name on each map
   D. Possibly be the one who does all the writing
   E. Encourage participation—make sure everyone speaks
   F. Listen/rephrase comments into statements, issues, etc.
      —don't repeat items
      —gently and politely encourage people to focus on their key point without too much elaboration
      —feel free to interrupt to clarify—ask for feedback on what you write on paper
   G. Be sure that unmappable items (insurance, ethics) get recorded
   H. Keep track of timing

V.   Encourage a new person to help present results to the entire group. Especially those items on the action map.

DIRECTIONS FOR SMALL-GROUP EXERCISES

Use the next hour or so, until 8:30 pm, to complete the four poster-map exercises. Before you start, be sure to appoint one or two group members as presenters. It will be their job to summarize your group's findings to everyone present toward the end of this evening.

Map 1 - The Unsecrets Map

The first map is for recording important things about Palmer Lake which are known only to a few or are recent proposals for development or change. This map is also used to record where group members live, work, or own property so there will be no surprises about people's interest.

Map 2 - The Good/Bad Map

This map is for recording how your group feels about Palmer Lake's assets and liabilities. Mark in green those things about Palmer Lake that are good—features that should be protected or built on. Mark in red those things that are problems or liabilities. If you wish you can just list assets and liabilities along the map's edge with arrows if the comment is site specific. However you decide to record your thoughts, do it quickly; it should be easy and fun.

Map 3 - The Ideal Map

This map is for recording your group's dream plan. Imagine your group is really in charge, with unlimited finances, no political or legal constraints, and no need to be considerate of other groups. Be imaginative and selfish in serving your own group's interests. This should be fun, though it may not be easy to just let loose, or to agree on what an ideal proposal is.

Map 4 - The Action Map

This map is quite different from all the others. It is intended for serious proposals of what should really be done in the next few years to ensure a sound and desirable community. You should consider the realities of politics, finance, law and other people's interests. It is chiefly from these action maps that the town council will develop actual proposals and their 1989 work program. If you have the time and patience, it would be good to make a list of priorities for your action proposals, perhaps putting them in three groups: highest priority, medium priority, low priority.

There will be a 15 minute break between the small group exercise and the group presentations. During this break, each group should bring their maps to the front of the room for display.

Shaping Proposals 8:45-9:15 p.m.

We will start by having each group briefly present its action proposals. Your group's presentation should be no longer then ten minutes and should ideally highlight the major objectives of your group's proposal. We will summarize the major action proposals on large newsprint as you present your ideas.

Palmer Lake Priorities 9:15-9:30 p.m.

Prior to leaving tonight's meeting, we want to get a sense of community priorities. To do this each of you will be given three voting dots. Place one or more dots next to the actions you wish to see the town work on in the upcoming year. You can put one dot on three different proposals or alternatively, place all your dots on your very favorite idea. You are free to leave at the end of the voting exercise or you can wait for the results.

Next Steps

At the first town council meeting in November, town council will report on the outcome of this town meeting and present preliminary recommendations on a strategy or strategies to pursue in the following year.

REFERENCES

Planning Methods

Community Development Dept., Tacoma, Washington (1986). *Do It Yourself—A Simple Approach to Neighborhood Improvement.*

Dandekar, Hemalata C. (1988). *The Planner's Use of Information—Techniques for Collection, Organization, and Communication.* Chicago: American Planning Association.

DeChiara, Joseph, and Lee Koppelman (1982). *Urban Planning and Design Criteria*, 3d ed. New York: Van Nostrand Reinhold.

Hester, Randolph T. Jr. (1984). *Planning Neighborhood Space with People*, 2d ed. New York: Van Nostrand Reinhold.

Smith, Herbert H. (1979). *A Citizen's Guide to Planning*, rev. ed. Chicago: American Planning Association.

Smith, Herbert H. (1983). *A Citizen's Guide to Zoning.* Chicago: American Planning Association.

Neighborhoods and Community Development

Boyte, Harry C. (1984). *Community is Possible—Repairing America's Roots.* New York: Harper and Row.

Clay, Phillip L., and Robert H. Hollister (eds.) (1983). *Neighborhood Policy and Planning.* Lexington, Mass.: D.C. Heath.

Hallman, Howard (1984) *Neighborhoods—Their Place in Urban Life.* Beverly Hills, Cal.: Sage.

Hetherington, Arlene (1989). "Rural Tourism Development: Finding, Preserving, and Sharing Your Community's Heart and Soul." *Pacific Mountain Review.* No. 2, pp. 5–8.

Rohe, William M., and Lauren B. Gates (1985). *Planning with Neighborhoods.* Chapel Hill, N.C.: University of North Carolina.

Taylor, Robert B. (ed.) (1986). *Urban Neighborhoods: Research and Policy.* New York: Praeger.

Warren, Rachelle B., and Donald I. Warren (1977). *The Neighborhood Organizer's Handbook.* Notre Dame, Ind.: University of Notre Dame Press.

Meetings and Group Process

Bertcher, Harvey J. (1979). *Group Participation Techniques for Leaders and Members.* Beverly Hills, Cal.: Sage.

Mill, Cyril R. (1980). *Activities for Trainers: 50 Useful Designs.* San Diego, Cal.: University Associates.

Community Surveys

Dillman, Don A. (1978). *Mail and Telephone Surveys—The Total Design Method.* New York: John Wiley.

Sudman, Seymour, and Norman M. Bradburn (1983). *Asking Questions—A Practical Guide to Questionnaire Design.* San Francisco: Jossey-Bass.

Weiss, Carol H., and Harry P. Harty (1971). *An Introduction to Sample Surveys for Government Managers.* Washington, D.C.: The Urban Institute.

Index

131